More Toasts to Dane Huckelbridge's *Bourbon*

"A witty and informative account of America's much-loved national beverage. Dane Huc... mash." —John Ba...

In Se...
IACP Cookbook

"Huckelbridge brings life to bourbon history."
—*Chicago Tribune*

"A mirthful, erudite appreciation of bourbon and its striking history. . . . [An] entertaining *tour d'horizon* of bourbon's birth and long, healthy life. . . . Huckelbridge knows his bourbon. . . . A snappy history of the popular spirit's rise and continued ascent." —*Kirkus Reviews*

"Informative. . . . What part hasn't bourbon played in American history? And what does that corn-based spirit say about this country's character? Huckelbridge has done a well-researched but laid-back job answering."
—*Memphis Flyer*

"Sure, you might have enjoyed a sip of bourbon before. Possibly on Bourbon Street. While eating a bourbon-glazed pork chop and wearing bourbon-scented aftershave. But until you read this 288-page historical treatise on the amber nectar, you'll never know the whole story."
—UrbanDaddy.com

"Dane Huckelbridge's debut book shows a mastery of conversational history and humor. He has written an accessible, breezy, and above all fun and informative history of America's national spirit. . . . A pleasure to read."
—*Washington Independent Review of Books*

"*Bourbon: A History of the American Spirit* traces U.S. history through one of the nation's favorite things, bourbon whiskey. From its origins—and the on-going battle over whether it was named after the Kentucky county or the street in New Orleans amongst other possibilities—to how the craft distilling movement is changing the look (and more importantly, taste!) of the market today, it is both completist without being boring." —TheDrinkNation.com

"Pour three fingers, crack open Dane Huckelbridge's *Bourbon,* and prepare to be taken along on a strange tale of moonshiners, gunslingers, hair-metal bands, and Brooklyn hipsters. The results: *smooth.*"

—Pagan Kennedy, *New York Times Magazine* columnist

"A three-hundred-year *tour de force* of our favorite corn liquor, as told by Dane Huckelbridge. From Columbus to Congressional resolutions to its evolution, Huckelbridge tells a story of bourbon and its ties to America that is almost as fun to read as bourbon is to drink." —CoolMaterial.com

"Although *Bourbon* is most certainly a history book, you won't even realize you're absorbing dates and events from as far back as 1500. That's because Dane Huckelbridge brings bourbon's birthplace, Kentucky and the rest of the U.S., to life with the sort of witty, character-rich zeal AMC writers might employ if they took over the History Channel. He argues that the whiskey backwoods farmers first developed in the 1700s isn't just America's spirit because it originated here. Bourbon embodies our collective spirit, too. It's hard to argue with that when he presents such a thorough, intoxicating case for it." —*Blade* (Toledo, OH)

"*Bourbon* the book, like bourbon the drink, has a special spirit. It is lighthearted, friendly, easy to enjoy. . . . Try it; you'll like it." —*Journal Star* (Lincoln, NE)

BOURBON

A HISTORY OF THE AMERICAN SPIRIT

DANE HUCKELBRIDGE

wm

WILLIAM MORROW

An Imprint of HarperCollins*Publishers*

Grateful acknowledgment is made to the following for the use of the photographs that appear throughout the text: Library of Congress (pp. 8, 23, 32, 34, 42, 53, 57, 59, 64, 66, 70, 74, 86 [top and bottom], 89, 91, 95, 102, 105, 112, 121, 134, 149, 157 [top and bottom], 166, 178, 180, 183, 186 [top and bottom], 190, 192 [top and bottom], 193, 197, 205, 215, 223, 244, 249, 259); University of Kentucky Libraries (pp. iii, 65 [top and bottom], 117, 125, 128, 139 [top and bottom], 144 [top and bottom]; Wikimedia Commons (pp. 6, 12, 16, 25, 49, 169); collection of the author (pp. 190, 219, 228, 261); Duke University Libraries Digital Collections (pp. 225, 241); Project Gutenberg/United States Department of Interior (p. 23 [top]); Mount Vernon Ladies' Association (p. 42); Blogspot.com (p. 60); Brown University (p. 77); Old Forester (p. 150); Old Crow (p. 152); *Life* magazine (p. 212); HarperCollins Publishers (p. 236); and Maker's Mark (p. 247).

Photograph on page 45 by Mark Gulezian, courtesy of Mount Vernon Ladies' Association. Photograph on page 252 © 2010 by Stace Carter.

HarperCollins books may be purchased for educational, business, or sales promotional use. For information please e-mail the Special Markets Department at SPsales@harpercollins.com.

A hardcover edition of this book was published in 2014 by William Morrow, an imprint of HarperCollins Publishers.

FIRST WILLIAM MORROW PAPERBACK EDITION PUBLISHED 2015.

Library of Congress Cataloging-in-Publication Data has been applied for.

ISBN 978-0-06-224140-5

HB 02.06.2023

It should therefore become the particular aim of the American distiller to make a spirit purely American, entirely the produce of our own country; and if the pure, unadulterated grain spirit cannot be rendered sufficiently palatable to those tastes, that are *vitiated* by the use of French brandy or Jamaican rum, let us search our own woods for an article to give it taste sufficiently pleasant for these depraved appetites.

Harrison Hall, *The Distiller*, 1818

The joy of bourbon drinking is not the pharmacological effect of the C_2H_5OH on the cortex but rather the instant of the whiskey being knocked back and the little explosion of Kentucky U.S.A. sunshine in the cavity of the nasopharynx and the hot bosky bite of Tennessee summertime—aesthetic considerations to which the effect of the alcohol is, if not dispensable, at least secondary.

Walker Percy

Old Jim and Jack are a hell of a couple fellers at night, but they ain't worth a damn the next morning.

Overheard by your Faithful Author at a family reunion

CONTENTS

PROLOGUE
America in a Bottle

I MMIGRANTS ESTABLISHED IT, pioneers expanded it, and capitalists spread its influence across the world. It made the West wild, the twenties roar, and rock music roll. George Washington was one of its Founding Fathers, F. Scott Fitzgerald its poet laureate, Hank Williams its cowboy bard. Rebellions were fought to free it, the Native Americans were brought low by it, religious zealots crusaded against it . . . and come Thanksgiving at the in-laws', millions whisper its praises.

The answer to this befuddling historical riddle? If you guessed the "United States of America," you are by no means wrong, although for our purposes "American whiskey" works just as well. Some small indication, perhaps, of how inextricably linked our national identity and national potation have become over three turbulent centuries of cohabitation and growth. The bourbon of today tastes very much like the oak-aged, corn-based spirit that, if legends are to be believed, the likes of Jacob Spears and Elijah Craig first barreled and dubbed "bourbon" before floating it down the Ohio River in the late eighteenth century. Only now, it's shipped by the ton in ocean freighters to every corner of the globe, with industry giants Jim Beam and Jack Daniel's* selling half their total output to overseas markets. The frontier stills of Kentucky and Tennessee still abound, cooking up sour mash and funneling its char-kissed progeny into bottles. But the massive distilleries that house them serve as the present-day engines in a multi-*billion*-dollar industry, producing some thirty million twelve-bottle cases a year for domestic and global consumption. Bourbon got big—just like America. But in certain less-obvious ways, just like America, it has also stayed small. And across the entire breadth of that historical journey, bourbon has been our constant and unfailing companion, a tad belligerent, yes, yet ultimately beloved. It's part of who we are as a nation.

But is it really so strange? Peculiar that an alcoholic beverage could maintain for so long such a crucial and inexorable hold over the collective consciousness of an entire people? After all, the Russians love their vodka, the Mexicans cherish their tequila, and the French, well, they've got a thing for full-bodied wines. Couldn't the argument be made that each civilization, irrespective of time or place, has some treasured vice that permeates the strata of its cultural mythology? Probably so. But in the case of bourbon whiskey, this rela-

---

* Author's Note: If you're going to enrage a sizable number of whiskey pundits along with the entire state of Tennessee, you might as well get it over with right away. After careful consideration and some deliberation, Tennessee Whiskey will henceforth be considered and referred to as a type of bourbon rather than a distinct spirit. Although the charcoal filtering of the Lincoln County Process does change its character slightly, and the moniker is indeed a clever marketing ploy, Tennessee Whiskey is essentially nothing more than a straight bourbon whiskey made in Tennessee (and contrary to popular misconceptions, bourbon does not require a Kentucky origin; it can be produced anywhere in the United States so long as corn content and aging restrictions are properly adhered to). Sorry, Uncle Jack. But somebody had to say it.

tionship takes on a unique, practically symbiotic dimension. Bourbon is not merely a cultural offshoot or by-product—a Coca-Cola with kick or a boozy Big Mac. Nor is it simply an omnipresent catalyst in a vast American experience. Bourbon whiskey, when carefully examined and held up to the light, *is* the American experience, distilled, aged, and sealed in a bottle. A version, captured in glass and brought down to miniature, of the very country that willed it into existence.

How so? Take a simple glance at bourbon's history, and the parallels become undeniable: a primary ingredient (corn) first cultivated by Native Americans. A distillation technique brought from Europe by immigrants. A recipe invented on the Western frontier. A spirit of rebellion born of social upheaval. A coming of age in the tumult of the Roaring Twenties. A global emergence in the postwar years. Sound familiar? From the Jazz Age to the Space Age, the Lost Generation to Generation X, bourbon has created our heroes and crippled our stars, fueled our imaginations and flummoxed our ideals. Simply stated, bourbon is the American Spirit, both blessing and bane served neat or on the rocks. To know its story is to know our own.

And this is how our story begins. . . .

1

Catalans, Corn Beer, and the Age of Discovery

I IS CUSTOMARY in any sort of whiskey narrative to begin with complex taste descriptions and Gaelic etymologies; it is standard fare in a bourbon discussion to commence with bucolic portraits of old Kentucky life. In this first chapter, you will find none of the above. Our tale—the story of bourbon and of America—begins several centuries before the first ragged Kentuckian set up a pot still outside his frontier cabin. No, we have to reach further back to the crucial "big bang" moment when the Old World first came face-to-face with the New. More specifically, to when the medieval science of distillation met a previously unknown indigenous grain. And to find such a moment, we must start somewhere a little unexpected: with hopped-up Aztecs and one hard-partying Catalan.

First, the Catalan. Allow us to present Senyor Ramon Llull. It was the year 1265, the Balearic Islands were freshly wrested from the Moors as part of Spain's incipient Reconquista, and young Ramon was living the life of a libertine, even by the laxest of moral standards.* Educated, wealthy, and incredibly well-connected (he was named head administrator to the royal family of Majorca, thanks to family ties), he had no compunction about indulging in the sensual pleasures of Mediterranean life, despite the pleadings of his wife and the mores of his social position. When not occupied with his relatively cushy job, Ramon wiled away his days writing dirty limericks and diddling the maids—more the stuff of reality TV shows and Rodney Dangerfield movies, it would seem, than religious conversions or scientific discoveries.

But quite unexpectedly, he suddenly saw the light, as explained in this excerpt from the *Vita Coaetanea*:

> *Ramon, while still a young man and Seneschal to the King of Majorca, was very given to composing worthless songs and poems and to doing other licentious things. One night he was sitting beside his bed, about to compose and write in his vulgar tongue a song to a lady whom he loved with a foolish love; and as he began to write this song, he looked to his right and saw our Lord Jesus Christ on the Cross, as if suspended in mid-air.*

As it turned out, a precoital midchoral sighting of a levitating, crucified Jesus proved impetus enough not only to shake Ramon away from his inveterate skirt-chasing and booze-hounding, but also to lead him right into the Holy Orders of Saint Francis. Spurred by his religious visions, the "born-again"

---

* Technically Ramon hailed from the Kingdom of Aragon, which was not yet part of a unified Spain. But Ferdinand said he was having a drink with Isabella next Friday, so let's see what happens . . . maybe he can Castile her heart.

It takes a lush: Ramon Llull, the father of hard liquor.

Ramon Llull left behind the comforts of his title and the pleasures of his vices to pursue a life of monastic solitude; and in that state of quiet contemplation, Ramon's intellectual faculties, previously stunted by carnal excesses, flourished.

Ramon Llull would spend the next nine years following his revelation writing treatises on botany, philosophy, linguistics, theology, mathematics (he is considered by many to be the founder of computational math), and, most important for the purposes of this book, alchemy. Alchemy—the precursor of modern chemistry—included techniques for concentrating liquids through distillation. And while the history of distillation goes back to the classical scholars of Alexandria, no one up until that point had applied those scientific principles to alcoholic beverages.* Or at least, not with the flaming passion or divine inspiration of the reformed party animal Ramon Llull, who, despite forswearing his rock star lifestyle, never completely abandoned his taste for the occasional tipple. In his journals, he is the first to pen specific formulas for "loosening" the alcohol from wine (for scientific purposes of course), and in his *Potestas Divitiarum*, he describes in workable detail a *retentorium*—a distilling condenser, the key component in the production of high-proof spirits. By applying some ancient technology to the popular drinks of his day, Ramon found that he could boil off the ethanol vapor, collect it in the neck of his makeshift still, and allow it to reliquefy upon cooling into something that packed a considerably stronger punch. It's impossible to know how Ramon reacted to that very first sip, but one can surmise, based on his continued and enthusiastic "research" into the topic, that he knew he had stumbled upon something amazing. And just like that, modern alcohol distillation came into being, courtesy of the freshly tonsured erstwhile lush, the friar Ramon Llull.

So what, exactly, did Ramon's discovery mean? Essentially, a viable method for producing hard liquor from fer-

---

* There is some evidence that early forms of alcohol distillation were also stumbled upon by other medieval scholars, particularly in Italy's Salerno School, where general distillery was an important subject of medieval academic study. Still (no pun intended), the formulas and techniques of Ramon Llull would ultimately prove to be those that intoxicated Europe for the next several centuries.

mented drinks low in alcohol. In the warmer south of Europe, this meant turning grape-based wine into primitive brandy. In the colder north, it meant transforming grain-based beer into a primordial sort of whiskey. And across the continent, it meant a faster and far more efficient way to get, in the courtly parlance of medieval times, absolutely shit-faced. Ramon's distillation techniques, along with the intoxicating aqua vitae they produced, would be spread rapidly

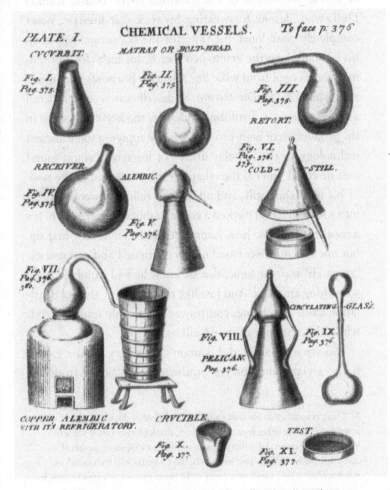

Early distillers had a full range of alembic stills at their disposal.

and enthusiastically by his fellow learned monks to wherever both Christianity and fermented alcoholic beverages could be found. And the New World, although unknown to continental European civilization during Ramon Llull's lifetime, was soon to become just such a place.

But wait, alcoholic beverages existed in the Americas before Columbus? Indeed they did. Distillation may require a still and a fermented drink, but fermentation requires only yeast and natural sugar—both of which could be found in North and South America long before any Genoese sailor mistook Jamaica for Japan. For the indigenous people of the Americas were masters of a domesticated crop with sugary potential: corn. And anyone who's read the ingredient label on virtually any processed American snack food knows just how deliciously sweet corn syrup can be.

Before immersing ourselves in the world of Native American corn beer, however, it is imperative to dispel several specious notions still lingering from earlier and less enlightened forms of Eurocentric thought: the ideas that Native Americans prior to European colonization were somehow "primitive," lived in small hunter-gatherer bands, had no knowledge of horticulture or agriculture, and were strangers to the potentially harmful effects of alcohol consumption. Lies, lies, lies.

Let's start with the very real phenomenon of Native American cities. Indigenous metropolises existed in the Americas with population levels that not only measured up to European capitals, but in some cases dwarfed them. While our old friend Ramon Llull was discovering new and more efficient ways to get his drink on in medieval Europe, the Mississippian civilization of central Illinois had an urban center at Cahokia with a population of some fifteen thousand people—comparable in size to London or Madrid at that time. By the sixteenth century, the Incan city of Cuzco would be home to more than one hundred thousand inhabitants, making it significantly larger than the London or Madrid of that era. And the grand-daddy of them all, the Aztec capital of Tenochtitlán, had between two hundred thousand and three hundred thousand rabid Montezuma fans hanging their hats there at night, making it one of the largest cities in the world at that time, and roughly *five times* larger than London or Madrid.

Tomahawks and teepees? Try public parks, sewage systems, sanitation departments, professional sports facilities, and a host of urban planning features virtually unheard of in Europe. That's not to say nomadic "hunter-gatherer" societies did not exist—they certainly did, both in the New World and the Old. But sprawling urban centers thrived right alongside them.

And the logical follow-up question—by what mechanism does one sustain so many people? The answer proved identical on both sides of the Atlantic: farming. More specifically, grain farming. Dense concentrations of human beings require dense concentrations of carbohydrates, of the kind generally found in starchy crops. In Europe, there was wheat, millet, oats, rye, and barley to power the metropolis. In pre-Columbian America, there was wild rice, potatoes, manioc, and, you guessed it, corn. Also known as maize. The domesticated native grain that provided the raw energy to run indigenous cities. Archaeological evidence indicates corn was first planted in Mexico's Balsa River valley some seven thousand years ago, a tamed and farmer-friendly version of the wild teosinte plant.* By 1500 BC, corn and its husbandry had spread out of Meso-

---

* Interesting side note: Scientists are still uncertain as to how the wild teosinte plant was first utilized, as its kernels were far tougher than modern maize, and extremely difficult to cook as a foodstuff. Some theorize that early Americans first consumed it in the form of popcorn.

america to become *the* staple crop for many native North and South Americans. Grown primarily on hillsides, and rotated just as it is today with bean crops to put nitrogen back in the soil, corn was not just the staple in the indigenous urban world, it was sanctified, worshipped, and even deified.* This corn worship occurred for all the obvious reasons mentioned, but for another, less obvious reason as well.

That reason, if you haven't figured it out already, was the very same one that so bewitched and bemused Ramon Llull an ocean away: alcohol. The magical sum of yeast plus sugar. What you get when you leave fruit juice or corn gruel out in the open a little too long. Native Americans did not have distilled spirits, but they were avid consumers of fermented alcoholic beverages, wines and beers made from maize, maguey, saguaro, sotol, honey, maple sap, persimmons, pineapple . . . you name it, they fermented it. The agave-based pulque of Mexico and the corn-based *chicha*† beer of South America are the descendants of such libations—simply brewed but stultifying concoctions that could lead their drinkers then, as they still do today, to dizzying new realms of consciousness. And as such, their consumption among many indigenous societies was carefully restricted and imparted with ceremonial regulation. The Aztecs used both pulque and corn beer as a form of Communion with their gods, in their most sacred and solemn of ceremonies. To abuse alcohol outside the sanctity of the temple was unpar-

---

* The Aztecs counted among their pantheon a specific maize god named Centeotl—try saying that five times fast.

† One common and rather ingenious ancient method for making *chicha* involved chewing balls of cornmeal and spitting them into a clay or stone pot for fermentation. This process allowed naturally occurring saliva enzymes to catalyze the transformation of cornstarch into yeast-friendly maltose sugar, and would forever redefine the term "backwash."

Drinking in Mesoamerica: She's had a few pulques
and corn beers, but she's cool to drive.

donable; to be publicly intoxicated a serious offense. Just
take a gander at what a citation for drunk and disorderly
conduct would have cost you in the Aztec world, as described
in the *Codex Ixtlilxochitl*:

> *Thus the drunkard, if he was plebian, had his hair*
> *cut publicly in the market square, and his house*
> *was sacked and torn down, because the law said*
> *that he who deprived himself of his good judgment*
> *was not worthy to have a house but could live in*
> *the fields like an animal; and the second time he*
> *was punished with death; and if he was a noble the*
> *first time that he was caught committing this crime*
> *he was punished with death.*

A rather stiff penalty, but effective for maintaining order
in a bustling city with a thirst for corn beer, and two American continents brimming with maize.

So here we are—arriving at last at that "big bang" moment
your Faithful Author promised the eager reader at the chapter's

onset. It's nearly the sixteenth century, all of Europe is getting bombed on Senyor Llull's hard liquor, indigenous Americans are shotgunning their Maize Lites during church, and . . . what's that in the distance? Three little Spanish* sailboats bobbing across the ocean, probing timidly at the horizon, ready to bring these two worlds crashing together.

America—and bourbon whiskey—are about to be born.

---

* At this point, we can indeed say "Spanish," as Castile and Aragon are united.

A Tale of Two Georges

T O OVERSTATE BOSTON'S importance in our nation's founding would be a daunting, if not flat-out impossible, task. From Plymouth Rock to Paul Revere, the city proved to be a patriotic incubator for the country's congealing identity, and a rallying point for its cohering spirit. But while the Boston chapter in the history books abounds with cathartic tea parties and inciting massacres, one story you're not likely to come across is that which occurred there on January 15, 1919—long after the last Revolutionary shots were fired at scampering redcoats. To understand the emergence of bourbon as America's spirit of choice, we must first take a closer look at what came before it, and the disaster that occurred on that day provides an excellent, and frankly rather jaw-dropping, analogy.

According to most accounts, it was an unusually pleasant afternoon in Boston's North End, with the temperature hovering around forty degrees, and the breezes off the harbor smelling faintly and freshly of sea spray and rime. Dockworkers and laborers took advantage of the mild weather, eating their lunches outside and discussing the gossip and news of the day, the native-born in the *r*-less argot of New England, and the immigrants in the more lilting inflections of Sicily and Donegal. They spoke no doubt of the uncertain promise of the upcoming baseball season (the Red Sox had taken the Series the year before, but the Babe was bitching about his salary again), the intricacies of local politics (Honey Fitz had been one crooked mick, but he was *their* crooked mick), and the terrors of combat—many among them had been coughing up mustard gas and trading blows with the Huns only months prior. They laughed with mouths full of coffee and sandwich, and they slapped one another on the back, and none of them had the faintest idea what was in store for them at approximately 12:41 p.m. on that pleasant day in the North End, only blocks away from where Paul Revere commenced his legendary ride, hardly a stone's throw from the tea party that helped jump-start a nation.

According to some witnesses, it began with a sound of metallic bursting akin to machine-gun fire—a sharp, staccato report that cleaved the stillness of the Boston afternoon. This was followed shortly after by an ominous rumble, a disconcerting wind of almost carnival sweetness, and a sight that made the Kaiser's machine guns seem rather quaint in comparison: 2.3 million gallons of molasses, traveling at thirty-five miles per hour, in a black tidal wave nearly three stories high. The lunch-break crowd watched in muddled horror as the fourteen-thousand-ton monster came surging down the narrow colonial streets, blasting apart buildings, ripping down bridges, and crumpling houses "as though they were made of pasteboard." Initial paralysis quickly turned to panic, and the men quite rightly decided to run for their lives. Some were lucky, but many more were not—the crushing wall of molasses proved too fast, and the lives for which they ran were snuffed and swallowed whole by the sticky tsunami.

Rum hangover: Boston in the wake of the molasses disaster of 1919. Twenty-one people were killed and 150 injured by the sticky black tidal wave of processed Caribbean cane sugar, the raw material for rum. During its heyday in the eighteenth century, rum production was a vital mainstay of the colonial New England economy. British taxation of imported Caribbean sugar threatened America's rum supply—and helped spark the Revolution, as well as the search for a native distilling ingredient that soon led to corn whiskey, aka bourbon. By 1919, the American rum industry was a shell of its former self and bourbon was long triumphant.

Once the syrup had settled and the tallies were taken, a clear picture emerged of just how quick and how deadly the flood had been. The Boston Molasses Disaster of 1919 killed 21 people and injured 150 more, making it one of the worst calamities in the city's history. And although few tangible traces of that fateful day in January remain, to this day some local residents claim that on especially warm afternoons, one can still detect the same disconcerting sweetness that pierced the air nearly a century ago, so thorough was the sticky-sweet saturation, so entrenched was the horror it left behind.

At this point, the inquisitive and discerning reader will no doubt be wondering what in the hell a freak twentieth-century molasses disaster has to do with bourbon whiskey in colonial America. A fair question that begs yet another: What in the hell was 2.3 million gallons of Caribbean molasses doing in Boston? For that deluge of cane syrup did not spring out of thin air, but rather from the ruptured holding tank of the Purity Distilling Company, a subsidiary of United States Industrial Alcohol. And while Boston and Bacardi are seldom uttered in the same breath these days, the fact that distillation on such a large scale was still taking place in the 1900s is a testament to the once-prominent role New England held in the triangular trade of the seventeenth and eighteenth centuries, not to mention a convenient reminder that the first spirit of our country was not whiskey at all, but the sugary by-product of British colonialism: rum. America at its onset was a colony of rum drinkers, beholden to both a liquor and a king foisted upon them. For whiskey to triumph, it would need to hack an identity all its own from the wilderness and declare its independence from foreign oppression. Luckily for bourbon, and for America, the Founding Fathers were epic boozers, and two different Georges—one whom you've likely never heard of, and another whose saucy wallet-sized portrait is very likely in your back pocket—were ready and willing to lead the way.

THERE'S ONE TASK historians and whiskey experts are notoriously reluctant to do: attach a firm date of birth to bourbon whiskey. Traditionally, bourbon has been dealt a fuzzy provenance hovering vaguely in the late eighteenth or early nineteenth century—the period in time when oak-aged corn liquor began to be called "Old Bourbon" after the frontier region where much of it was made. It is certainly a fair argument, with plenty of evidence to support it. But stating that bourbon, even in a primitive or inchoate form, did not exist before acquiring its moniker is a bit like saying America did not exist prior to the Declaration of Independence. There's always *something* there beforehand, and such things warrant not only mention but the credit they deserve. Which is why we're not only going to slap a birthday on bourbon a good century and a half before conventional estimates, we're also going to file our own version of a historical paternity suit—and make the controversial claim that the real father of our national spirit was not some philandering frontiersman or seductive Scots-Irish fellow, but an educated English gentleman by the name of Captain George Thorpe, Esq. True, his initial corn-based concoction probably bore little resemblance to the oak-aged contents of a modern bottle of Beam. And yes, his efforts ended in disastrous failure. But as with the Lost Colony of Roanoke that preceded him, the greatest of nations can have humble beginnings, and a disaster can be meaningful when it comes to making it in America.

ASK EVEN THE most distracted and paper airplane–inclined students of eighth-grade history, and they will tell you that the early English attempts at American colonization did not go well, so inept and misguided were those first sixteenth- and seventeenth-century ventures. Spain—England's primary European competitor at the time—already had a one-hundred-year head start on the colony game, and had been reaping the riches of the New World for decades, giving it a very real political and militaristic advantage back on its side of the Atlantic. And the French, well, they weren't far behind, either. Spurred by this obvious lag, the British Crown began issuing royal charters to private companies to settle the lands its first explorers had claimed—companies that, while skilled at white-collar paper pushing and contract wrangling, were severely lacking in the more blue-collar departments of swamp draining, Indian fighting, forest clearing, and buck hunting. Sure enough, plagues, massacres, famines—not to mention that whole Roanoke debacle—nearly ended the English colonial adventure in America. Nevertheless, thanks to a combination of cunning and cruelty exercised by the likes of John Smith and John Rolfe, a precarious little colony could be found in Virginia from 1607 onward, clinging for dear life to the banks of the James River.

And what did these early colonists, beset on all sides by ferocious wilderness and hostile natives, complain about? Not plagues, not massacres, not famines. But booze. Or more accurately, the lack thereof. Englishmen of that era were prolific drinkers, eschewing water unconditionally in favor of alcoholic drink.[*] And in the early seventeenth century, on the muddy, malarial banks of the James River, liquor stores were not exactly easy to come by. The most common complaint, according to a Virginia Company document dated July of 1620, was the lack of a "good drink, wine being too dear, and barley changeable and hard to grow." Basically, wine had a long enough shelf life to be shipped from Europe, but was astronomically expensive to import; beer could hypothetically be made in the colony, if it weren't for the fact that the European barley withered in the sweltering Southern heat—a fine conundrum, indeed. One resourceful colonial chemist by the name of Russell even went so far as to propose a sort of ersatz wine consisting of "saxifrage, liquorice boiled in water," making the claim that it would "make no man drunk." America's

---

[*]   In fact, most Englishmen of that era believed water to be practically poisonous to drink and detrimental to good health, a convenient excuse for downing alcoholic drinks . . . well, like water.

first root beer, perhaps, but hardly the hard stuff the colonists sought. The Virginia Company back in London responded the best they could, upping considerably their alcohol shipments between the years 1619 and 1620. They increased the shipment of beer from 5.5 tuns to 21 tuns, sack (sherry) from 11 gallons to 60 gallons, and aqua vitae (hard liquor) from 15 gallons to 60 gallons. But even that proved inadequate to wet the prodigious whistles of those very first colonials, with their inordinately large thirsts and no local source of liquor to call their own.

Which is where our first George comes in. In their efforts to curb the FUBAR factor and redirect their colonies toward something resembling profitability, the Virginia Company of London sent along with those booze shipments a fresh batch of company men to help get things back on track.* And among them was Captain George Thorpe, a Gloucestershire-born Gentleman of the King's Privy Chamber and onetime member of Parliament known for his generosity of spirit, his seemingly unlimited resources, his great faith in Providence . . . and his ability to cook up a good batch of hooch. For in addition to the tasks laid out for him in Virginia by both company and Crown—erect an iron foundry, install a silk plant, found a college, convert the Indians—he was also to captain the even more crucial task of establishing a liquor industry in America.† Getting the colonists a sustainable supply of alcohol to drink was an absolute imperative.

---

* Included among this new batch of royal charters was that issued to a little cargo ship called the *Mayflower*, which, in addition to Pilgrims, carried more beer in its holds than drinking water, and was destined for Virginia until North Atlantic gales blew it off course toward Cape Cod. Talk about a beer run gone sour!

† Perhaps one reason for Thorpe's selection may relate to his deceased manservant—it appears George had in his employ back in England one of the

Shortly after landing in Virginia in 1620, the middle-aged George Thorpe set up residence and assumed the role of deputy governor at the Berkeley Hundred plantation, where he expressed a refreshing sense of American optimism about his new surroundings, as evinced by this uncannily prescient missive to London:

> *No man can justly say that this country is not*
> *capable of all those good things that you in your*
> *wisdom and great charge have projected both for her*
> *wealth and honor and also all other good things that*
> *the most opulent parts of Christendom so afford.*
> *Neither are we hopeless that this country may also*
> *yield things of better value than any of these.*

George Thorpe settled into his new role with considerable ease, establishing a firm administrative handle on colonial affairs and focusing much of his attention on getting Virginia's primary cash crop—tobacco—out the door and ready for European markets. He also devoted his time to making America's incipient alcohol industry equally viable. The first and most obvious solution was wine. The English were hardly expert vintners, but grapes were not entirely beyond their ken, and grape juice was easy to ferment. The industrious George Thorpe set about planting as many wine-producing grapes as he could, laying down in a single season ten thousand vines for the lands he oversaw, and another three thousand for his own personal use—a herculean feat that earned him the praise of colonists and company alike.

---

young Indian men who came to London as part of Pocahontas's entourage, and was therefore relatively familiar with Native American culture in Virginia . . . although perhaps not as familiar as he should have been.

A first and noble stab at alcohol production, but still not sufficient. Grapes took time to grow, and wine was not nearly as familiar or pleasant to the Anglo-Saxon palate of that era as hearty drinks of simple grain. And while George did own a copper still capable of producing the same high-proof aqua vitae the company occasionally shipped their way, he still needed a fermented drink to run through it. All of which must have gotten the gears in Captain Thorpe's brain working, because while the beer- and whiskey-producing barley used back in the British Isles was in short supply in Virginia, the fledgling colony was positively rife with Indian corn. And a lightbulb, or at least an exceedingly radiant colonial oil lamp, must have lit up in George Thorpe's head, as the solution to Virginia's liquor woes became suddenly and obviously apparent. On December 19, 1620—the date of birth we're going to stamp, although not without some controversy, on bourbon's birth certificate—George Thorpe wrote the following in a letter to his buddy John Smyth of Nibley, with original seventeenth-century syntax preserved for effect:

Wee have found a waie to make soe good drink of Indian corne I have divers times refused to drinke good stronge English beare and chose to drink that.

And there you have it. Here's the moment that the basic elements of bourbon whiskey—a Native American grain and a European technique for condensing alcohol—were for the first time harmoniously joined. It's not known how George's corn-based liquor was initially received in the Virginia colony, although (and we are admittedly engaging in some playful historical speculation here) a letter to his employers across the pond penned on May 15, 1621, requested with considerable urgency sieves to make cornmeal and coopers to build

Fresh off the boat: Imported whiskey arrives on the wharfs of colonial Jamestown, Virginia. Fed up with irregular supplies of alcohol from England, some enterprising colonists started distilling New World grains.

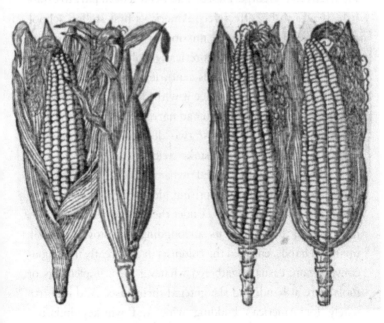

America's first colonists were quick to adopt Indian corn as a staple grain—and a key ingredient in locally distilled spirits. By definition, bourbon must be made from more than 50 percent corn mash.

barrels—both of which are indispensable, to this very day, for anyone engaged in the business of making bourbon.

Any big plans George may or may not have had for his primitive corn whiskey were quickly dashed, however, less than a year later. After a decade and a half of strained relations, local members of the indigenous Powhatan Confederacy, under the leadership of their ruthlessly efficient chief Opchanacanough, decided they'd had just about enough of the colonists. The Powhatan's gripes were multifarious and well-founded—the members of the Virginia colony had hunted off tribal game, stolen huge tracts of tribal land, and spirited off to England their princess (and Opchanacanough's own niece) Pocahontas, who would then die abroad of foreign disease. Hardly minor quibbles, to say the least. But the final straw seems to have been the very college at Henricus that George Thorpe had been sent in part to establish. It was to be, effectively, America's first Indian school, and although its intended mission of bettering the lives of Powhatan Indians was theoretically noble, the school was designed, like Indian schools centuries later, to erase Native American culture and replace it with that of the white man. And Opchanacanough, who had narrowly missed his chance to scalp John Smith almost two decades earlier, was not about to make the same mistake twice.

On March 22, 1622, the Powhatan Confederacy staged a coordinated massacre (or uprising, depending on one's viewpoint) of horrifying efficacy. Under the guise of peaceful visits, they entered the settlements surrounding Jamestown in small, unarmed bands, engaged the colonists in apparently innocuous conversation, casually gathered whatever farm implements or tools were at hand, and slaughtered their hosts. And unfortunately for America's budding wine and whiskey industry, George Thorpe was among their unlucky victims. He was struck down in the open while speaking to his Indian neigh-

The 1622 Powhatan massacre proved a disaster for
colonists, Indians, and whiskey lovers alike.

bors, whom he quite naively believed to be enthusiasts of whole-
sale assimilation. Possibly to send a clear message to the White
Fathers across the sea, his body was also mutilated in the most
grotesque of fashions—a sad finish for the father of bourbon.

By day's end, between 350 and 400 colonists—a sizable
chunk of the entire colony of Virginia—had been killed, and
the last thing on anybody's mind was wine or whiskey. But the
victory for the Powhatan Confederacy proved to be a Pyrrhic
one in the end. The Virginia Company in London responded
with a defiance that the fierce Opchanacanough could not
possibly have expected. Rather than abandoning the colony
and gathering up the surviving settlers, the company redou-
bled its efforts, sent more ships, and cracked down on indigenous settlements with a vindictiveness that would unfortunately
set the tone of Indian affairs for centuries to come. The attack
of the Powhatans struck a significant blow to both the colony

and its burgeoning bourbon market, but it did not destroy them. The proverbial seed, of America and its spirit, had been planted, borne out of the harsh realities of cultural conflict and frontier life. And both were there to stay.

Before closing this early chapter in bourbon's history and proceeding to the next, let's address the controversies surrounding the "birth" of American whiskey. Any paternity suit worth its salt has some healthy daytime drama to it, and our claim against George Thorpe is no exception. Because while there is little doubt that Captain Thorpe did indeed produce an alcoholic drink made of corn, there are some who question whether or not he actually had the equipment and know-how to distill it into whiskey*; and there are others who insist that even if he did engage in distillation, his liquor would have been far too raw to be considered even a primitive version of bourbon—fair contentions that a squinting bit of historical analysis can, hopefully, dispel. In the year 1634, almost twelve years after his untimely demise, an appraisal was taken on behalf of the Virginia Company in London of all the worldly possessions left in George Thorpe's ravaged little house. And sure enough, among that list of sundry items, the observant bourbon enthusiast will notice "a copper still, old" valued at three pounds of tobacco, and "an old case of bottles" valued at

---

* Is it strange that an Englishman such as Thorpe knew how to make whiskey? Not really. The English were avid consumers of aqua vitae, which is very nearly the same thing: Both mean "water of life," in Latin and Gaelic respectively. And although the Virginia colony was English in name, it had plenty of (Scots-)Irish settlers as well. As we'll soon see, the plantations in America were very much linked to the plantations in northern Ireland, with ships stocking up on supplies and men in Ireland before making the crossing, and indentured farmers from Ulster and the Scottish Lowlands filling the ranks. It's a safe bet that more than a few of them knew how to make whiskey, and would not have been shy about encouraging the one man with an old copper still to do so. As for the corn part, that was all George's idea.

four pounds of tobacco. Taken together, this is convincing evidence that George Thorpe was not only distilling alcohol from fermented beverages that came his way, he was distilling quite a bit of it. Given the obvious paucity of alcoholic options, not to mention the fact that the grapes he planted would not have had time to bear ripe fruit by the spring of 1622, it's only logical that he would have been distilling from the one source of alcohol he mentioned in his famous letter and possessed in large quantity, that being Indian corn. Evidence of his distilling success may even be found in a communiqué sent in the immediate aftermath of the massacre from the company in London to the governor of the Council in Virginia, attributing the disaster to the anger of Providence, who thus sought to punish the inhabitants "for enormous excesses in apparel and drinking." If a colony formerly starved for alcohol could suddenly consume so much of it—at least in the eyes of the company's administrators—as to warrant the wrath of a vengeful God, then perhaps George Thorpe and his thirsty tenants were turning out a lot more whiskey than anyone has imagined.

So assuming George was producing considerable quantities of corn whiskey from his old copper still, was what he put in all those bottles really bourbon? Well, not by modern aging standards, but then again, Jamestown in 1620 didn't bear much resemblance to a contemporary spring break at Virginia Beach, either. Both are early stages in the evolution of a nation and its spirit, and should be regarded as such. But even with that being the case, there is one other previously overlooked line in the late George Thorpe's postmortem inventory that deserves our thoughtful attention. Several lines below the bottles and copper still, there is a mention of the following:

> **A small runlett of Rosasolus and 3 runs. of Virginia, which were drunke out amonge the people that fetcht downe his goods.**

"Runlett" is an archaic loan word from Old French that means, basically, a wooden mini-keg used to store spirits. "Rosasolus" was a medicinal tonic made from alcohol and wild herbs. But the three mini-kegs of "Virginia" that the movers had no qualms about drinking? In the eighteenth century, one hundred years later, "Virginia Dram" would connote a type of peach brandy commonly enjoyed in the South, although it's unlikely that was what George Thorpe was making—the peach was first brought to Virginia by George Minifie in 1623, a year after Thorpe's deadly pow-wow. The more plausible interpretation, we will contend, is one that whiskey historians have previously ignored. In the early seventeenth century, "Virginia" was used by English colonists as a synonym for "Indian." Anything or anyone indigenous could be termed as such. The Powhatan girls who accompanied Pocahontas to England were referred to as "Virginia maidens." George Thorpe himself called his Powhatan servant his "Virginia boy." Wouldn't it make sense to dub a spirit made from Indian corn "Virginia" liquor? If that was the case, the movers in question who drank from George's wooden barrels in 1634 would not only have downed some of the world's first corn whiskey, they very well may have savored a deliciously mellow, barrel-aged, twelve-year-old small batch bourbon, crafted personally by the spirit's originator—a delicious prospect, indeed.

THE FIRST SETTLERS in Virginia may have distilled a primitive form of bourbon into existence, but if you're expecting men in powdered wigs and knee breeches slugging back Wild Turkey, expect to be disappointed . . . or at the very least, severely underwhelmed. Whiskey made from both corn and rye certainly did exist in seventeenth- and early eighteenth-century America—an inventory of a general store in York County, Virginia, from 1667 mentions ten gallons of the stuff under the guise of local "aqua vitae," and an expedition to the Blue Ridge Mountains led by Alexander Spotswood in 1716 included "Irish usquebaugh"* among its many alcoholic provisions. But mentions of whiskey during this period are few and far between. This is due in part to competition from the considerable array of ciders, brandies, and ales favored regionally in the colonies, but it is more directly tied to the fact that American whiskey in that era was utterly and unequivocally dominated by politics. British colonial policy was all about protecting the rum business. Colonial whiskey makers barely stood a chance.

The first major distilleries in England's American colonies opened in the 1640s, in Boston and New York.† Their initial attempts at producing a viable local spirit were indeed grain-fueled, as the environs of both cities were rich in farmland. This changed quickly, however, when strict regulations were set on colonial grain usage, and another, far sweeter option was set upon the table. For Mother England didn't just have colonies on the Eastern Seaboard; she had Caribbean islands flying the Union Jack as well. Those islands were home to plantations powered by African slaves who chopped cane to make sugary molasses. Spurred by the timeless economic laws of supply and demand, a cruel trade

---

* The word "whiskey" is actually derived from this older Gaelic term for the hard stuff. Both corn and rye whiskeys were frequently referred to as "usquebaugh" in early America.

† Technically New York was still a Dutch colony at the time of its first distilleries, but the city wouldn't stay that way for much longer. The Dutch influence would survive, however, in the many windmill-friendly names that still dot the five boroughs to this day. Broadway, Brooklyn, the Bronx, Harlem, Coney Island—they all owe their origins to Old . . . well, actually New Amsterdam.

triangle developed between those three points, with the hypotenuse linking New England and Africa representing the alcoholic portion of the deal. Rum is in its essence nothing more than distilled fermented molasses, and in the barter-heavy economy of the day, it turned out to be an excellent form of currency. British merchants and their New World affiliates learned to exploit the disparate, far-flung demands of foreign colonial markets, making fortunes by shipping their glut of Caribbean molasses to the distilleries of New York and New England, converting it upon arrival into precious barrels of rum, shipping the rum to West Africa to be traded for slaves, and returning shortly thereafter with a hold of human cargo bound for the hell of Caribbean and Southern plantations. A vicious cycle, it should be added, in the most literal sense of the term.

Which brings us back to our saccharine tsunami of molasses that engulfed Boston at the beginning of the chapter. As previously hinted, the distillery that in 1919 unleashed that sugary beast upon Beantown was part of the lingering legacy of almost three centuries of rum distillation in New England, dating back to 1648, the year the first rum distillery was established in Massachusetts. Rum exploded onto the American colonial scene, growing in both popularity and production over the century that followed. And what wasn't shipped abroad was enthusiastically consumed at home. By 1717, there were twenty-seven rum distilleries in Boston; a mere decade later, that number had increased to forty. Add into the mix the Caribbean rum that was soon brought in to keep up with American demand, and you're talking about a veritable flood of inexpensive liquor, produced both domestically and abroad. Between 1700 and 1709, New York received a whopping 526,000 gallons of it, with Boston and Barbados the primary providers. An English visitor to the colonies from that era called rum "the comforter of their Souls, the Pre-server of their bodys, the Remover of their Cares and Pro-moter of their Mirth." Aside from those tasks just mentioned, it also spawned taverns, swindled Indians, fueled pirates, and started to put some interesting ideas into these young Americans' heads.

When British interests in the Caribbean became concerned that American-made rum was becoming a little too competitive with theirs, they lobbied in favor of the Molasses Act of 1733, a mandate that doubled the duty paid by Americans on British molasses. Rather than accepting the terms and going out of business as their limey competitors hoped, the American distillers simply ignored the edict and began buying smuggled molasses directly from foreign nations and privateers—an act of direct, illegal defiance on the part of a feisty new nation that was starting to give England the most middle of its fingers.

Rum fever reached its delirious peak in the middle of the eighteenth century. Rum distilleries could be found in every major city of the Eastern Seaboard, producing a staggering domestic total that was further augmented by imports. It's almost impossible to say how much whiskey was being produced then by the odd backwoods farmer or indentured servant, but any estimate would pale in comparison to the amount of molasses-based alcohol pickling the collective liver of our original thirteen. By 1770, the 140-some rum distilleries of the colonies were producing more than five million gallons of rum on their own, and importing another four million from the Caribbean. Some estimates put the average amount consumed by an adult male of that era at three pints a week. Rum, it seemed, had become the American drink, thanks to its colonial master an ocean away. And as long as the cheap rum kept coming, America, although not entirely content with British rule,

An early American barroom: Whiskey may not be at the top
yet—it's listed sixth on the sign behind the bar, beneath rum,
brandy, and gin—but it's on the scoreboard and gaining fast.

was at least willing to suffer it. Why tinker around making whiskey, when rum could be had for next to nothing? A good question, and one that several hundred thousand redcoats were soon to answer.

THE TEA, STAMP, and Quartering Acts have received considerable ink in American textbooks over the years, in dense, easily forgettable paragraphs that deem them the impetus of the American Revolution. Curiously absent from that list is the law that arguably did more to fan the flames of revolution than the others combined: the Sugar Act. Enacted in 1764, it granted the Royal Navy the right to board and confiscate any vessel suspected of carrying contraband molasses or illegally imported alcohol—actions that infuriated not just your common colonial rummy, but the men who in time would become the Founding Fathers of our country.* For while we all have come to know them as enlightened, liberty-loving sages, far less is heard about their great love of liquor. The soon-to-be General Washington shipped in Madeira by the literal boatload, drinking a bottle or five whenever he had the chance. Sam Adams was a brewer, pounding back tankards of ale as if they were teacups. Ben Franklin was a boozehound (in addition to coozehound), and when not trolling for Parisian trollops he was craving French cognac. Why, even Paul Revere himself was said to have drunk enough rum just prior to his famous midnight ride to make "a rabbit bite a bulldog." These were

---

* Even John Adams would admit: "I know not why we should blushingly confess that molasses was an essential ingredient in American independence.... Many great events have proceeded from much smaller causes." Wise words from a lifelong drinker famous for downing hard cider and beer before breakfast.

not teetotalers by a long shot.* But they didn't just enjoy downing their imported potations; many also had big money invested in alcohol's manufacture and distribution. One such gent was a fellow you may have heard of by the name of John Hancock. He enlarged his purse over the years by putting his famous signature to dockets of his liquor-based importation business. When his aptly named ship *Liberty* was impounded by the British in 1768 for smuggling alcohol, Bostonians reacted by storming the ship during a riot and "liberating" it of its cargo—a wicked good time, any way you look at it. This event, preceding the Boston Tea Party by half a decade, was what truly ignited the fuse of the Revolutionary spirit.

To further protest this gross injustice, Americans throughout the colonies initiated a boycott of imported British goods, even though it meant turning away their much-beloved imported alcohol. It was a trying ordeal, particularly in 1769 when a ship chock-full of the best British brewing malt coasted temptingly into Philadelphia, but their resolve held firm. The colonists' determination to fight the injustices of intoxication without representation proved far greater than their thirst, and a new movement was born to wean America from its rum addiction once and for all—it was time for thirteen British colonies to start thinking of themselves as one united, booze-producing nation independent of

---

* Still not convinced? Check out the bill for the party that the Founding Fathers threw at Philadelphia's City Tavern in 1787 to celebrate the signing of the Constitution: They drank sixty bottles of claret, fifty-four bottles of Madeira, twenty-two bottles of porter, twelve bottles of beer, eight bottles of whiskey, eight bottles of hard cider, and seven bowls of rum punch. Divided among the fifty-five men in attendance, that's . . . well, a lot of liquor. Throw in the broken glasses and decanters also mentioned in the bill, and you're talking about one smashing party.

her transatlantic enabler. A list of practical tips to do just that was penned by Mr. Benjamin Franklin himself, in his famous *Poor Richard's Almanack*:

> First, *for making good wine of our own wild Grapes*. Secondly, *for raising Madeira Wine in [this] province*. Thirdly, *for the Improvement of our Corn Spirits, so as they may be preferable to Rum. And this seems very material; for as we raise more Corn than the English West-India Islands can take off, and since we cannot now well sell it to the foreign Islands, what can we do with the Overplus better, than to turn it into Spirit, and thereby lessen the Demand for West-India Rum, which our Grain will not pay for?*

Ben didn't just make a good and patriotic point—he, in a mere smatter of words, described what would become the destiny of bourbon and America for the next two hundred years.

On April 19, 1775, the first shots were fired at the Battles of Lexington and Concord; on July 4, 1776, as everyone knows, the Declaration of Independence was adopted by the Continental Congress. And for the first time since the days of old George Thorpe, an American couldn't get a dang ol' drop of foreign liquor if he tried, because those jolly chaps in the Royal Navy were blockading every major port in the land. Suddenly, Benjamin Franklin's idea of making our own native liquor from our own native corn started to sound like a darn good one, even after our independence was won. America became the world's newest nation, and bourbon whiskey, right alongside her, the world's newest spirit—a drink we could claim unambiguously as our own.

Your average corner bar circa the American Revolution,
when whiskey, like the country itself, was just catching on.
This tavern sign hung in Walpole, New Hampshire.

IF YOU'VE EVER wandered the monumental streets of our nation's capital, if you've ever gazed in awe upon the breadth of the Delaware, if you've ever been to a down-market strip club and attempted to convert the entire contents of your wallet into smaller yet far more fungible denominations, then you're already on a first-name basis with the second George of this story: George Washington. Founding Father, Revolutionary War hero, strapping general, first president, and . . . wait for it . . . major whiskey distiller. Believe it or not, George Washington played a vital role in the emergence of both bourbon and rye whiskey in America, an important point often overlooked by scholars and laymen alike. The fact that he has occasionally been depicted as no great friend to whiskey stems from his role in quelling the Whiskey Rebellion, which we will tackle later, and by a few misappropriated quotes used by temperance leagues a full century after the fact. Truth be told, George loved his drink; shipped wines, brandies, and ales in from England by the crateful; and thanks to his alliance with an industrious Scottish immigrant, became one of the leading whiskey distillers in early America, introducing what had been a fringe drink of frontiersmen to Virginia's planter class. G.W. was, as it turns out, an original Founding Father of bourbon whiskey.

George's first lesson on the mass transformative potential of alcohol was imparted to him long before the Stars and Stripes was a glimmer in Betsy Ross's eye. In 1755, a young George Washington ran for the Virginia House of Burgesses, executing a feebly managed and poorly planned campaign that failed to do the one thing every crafty politician learns in Civics 101: get the voters liquored up. He lost by a resounding margin, garnering a mere 40 votes against the winner's 271. God knows what his opponents were serving, but it was certainly better than nothing. You see, money ruled campaigns in those days, too—it's just that political war chests were spent on booze rather than TV spots. In 1758, when George decided to run again, he corrected his previous oversight, distributing to prospective voters 47 gallons of beer, 34.5 gallons of wine, 70 gallons of rum punch, and a fair quantity of cider and brandy as well. It worked out to half a gallon of alcohol per vote—and he won. Washington had learned his lesson and learned it well, generously applying it to soldiers later in his career. In 1777, in the bloody midst of the Revolution, he would remark that "there should always be a Sufficient Quantity of Spirits with the Army. . . . In many instances, such as when they are marching in hot or Cold weather, in Camp in Wet, on fatigue or in Working Parties, it is so essential, that it is not to be dispensed with." He would further invite the admiration and loyalty of his troops with a general order to supply those under his command with "four gallons of rum, made into punch, every day," giving a whole new meaning to the phrase "locked and loaded."

The events of the Revolution and his subsequent presidency did not hamper George's love of drinking and toasting, but they did keep him away from his beloved Mount Vernon plantation in Virginia. When he eventually "retired" in 1797, he returned to the rolling fields and tended forests of his estate, very much looking forward to the subdued life of a country gentleman. In order to ease the transition, he took on a Scotsman by the name of James Anderson to act as something of a farm manager around Mount Vernon, overseeing its business dealings and day-to-day affairs. And Mr. Anderson's Scottishness is a matter of no small importance. Born and raised near the village of Inverkeithing, approximately fifteen miles north of Edinburgh, the man knew his scotch whiskey. In fact, the farms he had previously

The Pounding Father: George Washington celebrating the end of the Revolution and his retirement from the army on December 4, 1783, at Fraunces Tavern in lower Manhattan.

managed in Scotland sold the vast bulk of their grain to a distilling conglomerate owned by the Stein and Haig families, who produced roughly 50 percent of the country's scotch whiskey. Anderson's very reason for emigrating was due in large part to an act passed by the English Parliament in 1788 to reduce competition from Scottish distilleries, a punitive measure that drove scotch makers and grain farmers into bankruptcy. James Anderson moved to America, was put in touch with George Washington, and, upon seeing the estate he was soon to manage, wasted no time in suggesting they set up a whiskey distillery not unlike the ones he knew from the Old Country. Evidently, you can take the boy out of Scotland, but you can't take the scotch out of the boy.

Only one small problem: Barley was not well suited to Virginia's hot climate; corn and rye fared considerably better. And Mount Vernon produced a great deal of both, the result of a transition from tobacco to grain that George Washington had encouraged as early as the 1760s, when unstable tobacco prices and the institution of slavery both began to discomfit the hereditary planter. James, no doubt after scratching his Highland head and consulting with a few local distillers familiar with New World whiskey, realized that what he had done back in Scotland with barley he could just as easily do at Mount Vernon with its surfeit of corn.

George Washington, however, was a tad bit skeptical. To him, corn and rye whiskeys were still the belligerent domain of hardscrabble squatters in the backwoods of America, people he had gotten to know all too well during the Whiskey Rebellion five years earlier. Not the best liquor, perhaps, for Virginia aristocrats. But James Anderson was persistent, and won George over with his enthusiasm for the idea, and his promises of good returns on the investment. Washington went along with the plan, writing on January 8, 1797, "I consent to your commencing a distillery, and approve of your purchasing of the Still, and entering of it." This endorsement did not come without some reservations, however, as he also expressed concerns over "idlers" dropping by and "robbing the Still"—George Washington had experienced great difficulties prior to this with various overthirsty tenants, and wished to avoid such complications at all costs.

But it was enough to get James Anderson started. Together with his son John, he set up a distillery with five working copper stills, each of which held more than 100 gallons, and a malt house and grain kiln, to boot. Over the course of the next year, while perfecting the recipe, they would produce some 600 gallons of good, drinkable whiskey; by 1799, that number would grow exponentially to 10,500 gallons, sold at sixty cents per gallon for their "common" whiskey, and nearly a dollar for the more premium product that had been distilled as many as four times. Deliveries were made for the most part in bulk, going out to many of the region's most prestigious planters and merchants. Washington was a well-connected man to say the least, not to mention the father of a nation, so when word of his whiskey got around, people snatched it up. The former president would even write to his own nephew, "Two hundred gallons of Whiskey will be ready this day for your call, and the sooner it is taken the better, as the demand for this article (in these parts) is brisk."

George and James made a good team, and the latter's notions of making American whiskey were incredibly good ones. When George Washington shed his mortal (and copper distilling) coil on December 14, 1799, he was one of the largest whiskey producers in America. A consolatory twenty-nine gallons of his Mount Vernon whiskey were delivered by his overseer to the grieving funeral party, and the lead lining of his coffin was lovingly hammered out by the very same coppersmith who had made for him his original copper stills three years earlier—not a bad way to go for a Founding Father of America's spirit.

A question that the curious reader, skeptical scholar, and shrewd marketing exec must surely be asking, however— what did George Washington's whiskey taste like, and how would it have compared to modern bourbon? As with our first George, since none of the original recipe survives, we must rely rather heavily on circumstantial historical evidence. But with a little thoughtful analysis and some creative speculation, we can almost smell a glass of Washington's whiskey passed beneath our historical noses.

The whiskey produced at Mount Vernon was admired in

In the late eighteenth century, Mount Vernon became one of the largest
commercial whiskey distilleries in America.

A re-creation of George Washington's original whiskey stills at present-day
Mount Vernon. After the war, Washington planned to settle into the quiet life
of a gentleman farmer and distiller—fortunately for the country, he returned to
public service to save the Constitutional Convention and, of course, serve two
presidential terms.

its day, and it probably tasted not so different from the bourbon and rye whiskeys of today. It is known that Washington's cooperage supplied barrels to the distillery, and that George, a lifetime drinker of brandy, rum, and wine, was more than familiar with the positive and calming effects wood-aging could have upon raw and fiery alcohol—he frequently commented on the virtues of his favorite "old" spirits, and happily received from the designer of the U.S. Capitol, William Thornton, a shipment of aged rum that had obtained its rich color and flavor from "standing in Oak casks" for a number of years. Given his appreciation for the aging process, Washington surely subjected his personal supply of distilled spirits to similar treatment, although considering the short lifespan of his distillery, most of the whiskey he sold would have been aged by the customer rather than the distiller. As the final product was distilled purely from grain by a Scotsman in possession of a grain kiln and familiar with scotch making, and since it likely received at least some oak-aging, we can surmise that Washington's whiskey was probably a smidgen rawer and smokier than the common bourbon labels we know today, and spicier, too, thanks to the high rye content in the mash bill, but otherwise very much the same.

As to whether or not the Mount Vernon whiskey could have been considered actual bourbon by today's stringent standards (whiskey that's made primarily from corn and aged in fired oak), it's difficult to say with exactitude, although the evidence supports the conclusion that if it was not bourbon, it was something fairly close. The firing of barrels was a practice common to rum distillers, and mentions of it go back to 1781, so it's not unlikely that a whiskey distillery would have engaged in the same practice. As for the mash bill—the recipe for the grains involved—sadly, James Anderson's secret was not preserved for posterity. But based on records of grain allotments for the distillery, it is clear that corn and rye were both used extensively, meaning that the whiskey could have been considered rye or bourbon, depending on the percentages.

Today's rye and bourbon generally contain both grains in their mash bills, with the actual designation depending on which grain can claim the majority. Some archaeologists and historians have suggested that since more rye was sent to the distillery than corn, the likely mash bill contained both corn and rye, with the latter in greater abundance, making the final product more of a rye whiskey than a modern bourbon. This is a possible scenario, but neglects the experimental aspect of the distillery: James Anderson was known to employ all sorts of tasty tricks, and in his attempts at creating a serviceable whiskey, also tinkered around with cinnamon seasonings, wheat spirits, flavored brandies, and a host of other combinations, winning and not. Recipes would have varied depending on the availability and cost of grain, with rye and corn alternating depending upon the season. James surely made whiskey using both rye and corn, at various times in combination, and at other times separately. And your Faithful Author would wager a bottle of Pappy Van Winkle's that when the mash bill leaned in the direction of corn, and the result was left to spend some time in the barrel, what Virginians were sipping was honest-to-goodness bourbon.

And so, in grand form, the colonial chapter of America and American bourbon comes to a close. At its commencement, during the earliest years of the seventeenth century, the American Spirit was but a fragile thing, an ambiguous, wind-tossed flame barely hanging on beneath George Thorpe's little copper still in a fragile settlement in the New World. By the close of the colonial period, however, that ethereal ember had become something bold, unique, and fiercely our own. With George Washington's death in 1799,

George Washington's distillery ledger,
with separate columns for corn and rye.

on the eve of the nineteenth century, so passed with him many of the vestiges of British hegemony, a fact indisputably illustrated by what we, as a people, chose as our drink. In 1774, with Revolution brewing and America only just beginning to assert its independence, rum accounted for more than 90 percent of the distilled spirits consumed in America; in 1790, with independence won, whiskey began to catch up, accounting for one third of total spirits consumed. And by 1810, a decade after President Washington bid the American firmament his final farewell, and with America on firm footing, whiskey had overrun its competition completely, occupying the 90 percent stake rum had once held on to. The United States of America was at last a real country, and whiskey made from domestic grains its much-preferred drink. And with the triumphant severance of British ties, not to mention the Franco-American boondoggle of the Louisiana Purchase, the future of our nation—and our liquor—quite suddenly seemed boundless, and utterly undefined.

The only thing missing?

A tribe of hog wild, weapon-slingin', whiskey-lovin', Anglo-Celtic cusses to come a-hootin' and a-hollerin' all doon' the hill and give our spirit a little frontier fire.

3

The Scots-Irish Are Coming, the Scots-Irish Are Coming!

GLOAMING HAD ALREADY begun to seep into the hollows, and lightning bugs were making their presence known when things turned sour on the banks of Blackberry Creek on August 7, 1882. Not that it was totally unforeseen—Election Days in those parts were always ribald, rambunctious affairs, with the menfolk eager to celebrate the democratic rights that many of their own great-granddaddies had so valiantly fought for and won. Emotions ran high, old gripes were stirred anew, and the whiskey flowed freely. Beneath the quaint, church-picnic coating of homespun and calico ran mountain blood made hot by its history, and even hotter by that ol' corn in a jar. And the names of the men swigging it on this particular Election Day were of no help either. They mostly ended with Hatfield or McCoy.

What began with a petty squabble about a stolen fiddle— Tolbert McCoy accused a Hatfield by the name of "Bad 'Lias" of never having paid the $1.75 he owed him for it—grew by dint of corn whiskey and lingering grudges into nothing short of a bloodbath. Mountain men of that era seldom left their cabins without an article capable of dispensing death, and they possessed no fear of doing so when their safety, honor, or rights as men were impinged upon. It's what had made them such terrifying soldiers in the Revolution a century before, and even more terrifying drunks on the banks of that crick one hundred years later; these were not men one would want to ever slight or wrong. The constable was initially able to limit the fight to nothing but fists, but when Ellison Hatfield rose from a whiskey-fed slumber to hurl a few cusses at the riled-up Tolbert, weapons and all hell both broke loose.

By the drunken melee's end, Ellison had been opened and bled twenty-six times by a knife and once by a pistol, and lay on the packed earth nudging toward death. Tolbert and Pharmer, the McCoy boys responsible for Ellison's wounds, fled into the woods, only to be captured in the laurel by two justices of the peace . . . both of whom wore, in addition to a badge, the surname of Hatfield.

Three days and three nights of vendetta ensued. The Old Testament in Tug Fork was not taken lightly—eye for an eye, tooth for a tooth. When the grievously wounded Ellison Hatfield finally gave up the ghost on the ninth of August, the code of the mountains demanded swift retribution. Tolbert and Pharmer McCoy were found not long after, on the Kentucky side of the border that the Tug River made. Their bodies were riddled with bullets, their heads, both of them, nearly shot off, and their blood made to shimmer in the cold light of lanterns, spattered across the pawpaw bushes to which their corpses had been tied.

In the decade-long explosion of violence that followed,[*]

---

[*] The end of the feud is generally assigned to the 1890s, although the somewhat amusing argument can be made that the bad blood continued right on up until the 1979 taping of the popular television game show *Family Feud*, which featured representatives of both the Hatfields and the McCoys, as well as a live pig.

trials would be held, men would be hanged, state militias called in—even the Supreme Court would be thrown into the fray, those befuddled and bespectacled justices surely wondering just who on earth were these people, capable of turning a minor tiff involving whiskey and fiddles into a national debacle.

Well, if whiskey, fiddles, and ancestral blood feuds sound reminiscent of an emerald isle across the sea, you're not far off. Some simple genealogy reveals the source of the trouble. Tolbert and Pharmer McCoy, the two McCoy boys who introduced Ellison Hatfield to his maker, were the sons of Randolph McCoy; Randolph McCoy was the son of John McCoy; and John McCoy was the son of William McCoy, a plantation Protestant born in Ireland in 1750, who set sail for

Appalachian Mountain clans like the Hatfields took both their whiskey and their feuds quite seriously.

America around the time of its independence and settled on the edge of the freshly opened frontier.

So who are these people? They're some of the first immigrants in a nation of immigrants, the first frontiersmen in a country defined by the frontier, and generally, just some of the biggest bad-asses you'll ever meet. They're one of the most colorful and enigmatic people to ever straddle a hyphen, and they came to America searching for what they could not find in Europe: religious freedom, land to call their own, and a decent bar with some Hank in the jukebox. In the hills of Kentucky, they found all of the above (well, they'd have to wait a bit for the Hank tunes), not to mention a cheap new grain to run through their copper. Bourbon may have taken its first teetering steps during the early days of the colonial era, but it took a people as handy with a still as they were with a hoe or a gun to tame the frontier and create the American Spirit we know today.

Say, have you met the Scots-Irish?

HISTORICALLY, IRELAND AND Scotland may not have been at the head of the class when it came to chemistry, but they were quick studies at distilling whiskey. Only a century or two after Ramon Llull first described the secrets of distillation, fans of his process were making their own Gaelic version of his discovery—known locally as *uisce beatha*—in both countries. Whiskey's spread to the Celtic hinterlands was due primarily to the peripatetic habits of Ramon's fellow monks, and its reputation as a medicinal cure-all. Said monks discovered quickly, however, that whiskey could do more for a party than it could for the plague. And since grain was far more plentiful than grapes in the cold, dark north, they didn't have much of a choice. It was either strong whiskey or weak ale when it came time to tip the wrist, and the peoples of both nations were more inclined toward the former. In 1405, to wit, a "Richard Magranell, chieftain of Moyntyreolas, died at Christmas by taking a surfeit of aqua vitae," according to the Mageoghegan version of the Irish *Annals of Clonmacnoise.* The learned editor of the classic text goes on, with typical Irish wit and candor, to mention that "it was not *aqua vitae* to him, but *aqua mortis.*" Exactly one century later in the hard-drinking town of Edinburgh, a decree was issued restricting the practice of whiskey distillation solely to the town's barbers. What the Hibernians and Caledonians lacked in good judgment or hairstyles, they more than made up for in daring and dash.

The majority of the early stills operating in Scotland and Ireland were small and portable copper affairs, simple pot stills probably not so very different from the one George Thorpe used to produce his corn-based aqua vitae in Virginia. But that doesn't mean it was all cottage industry— whiskey became big business in the Old World long before it did in the New. Bushmills, the celebrated Irish whiskey, received a license to distill on a large scale in Antrim way back in 1608. And the folks at the Scotch distillery of Kennetpans—whiskey makers who the Scotsman at Mount Vernon had once known quite well—were running stills of a whopping 1,200 gallons by the late eighteenth century, dwarfing even the largest stills George Washington ever used. Needless to say, in the realm of distillation, Scotland and Ireland were way ahead of the curve. These were whiskey lands, occupied by whiskey-drinking people; it ran through their veins and their pot stills alike, and they would take a good measure of both wherever they went—especially America.

Now, the daunting although not impossible task of ascribing a definite identity to a people whose very history and nature render them indefinite: the Scots-Irish. Contrary to what even those of Scots-Irish extraction may tell you, they were never simply a frontier mélange of Scottish and Irish immigrants. In fact, for most of their history, these feisty Protestants have been sworn enemies of the shillelagh-swinging Catholics who fled the Potato Famine and the bagpipe-blowing Highlanders who escaped the clearances of English occupation.

The frontier part, however, is correct. Not just in the modern sense of "frontier," with its connotations of log cabins and corncob pipes, but also in the word's original Latinate meaning: "border." Because long before the migration path of these people took them first to the Ulster plantations of northern Ireland and later the mountain wilderness of America, they called the Lowlands border country between Scotland and England home. Neither entirely Celtic nor dominantly Anglo-Saxon, they instead occupied the nebulous gap separating the two, creating a language, lifestyle, and culture that combined elements of both. They used Old English words like "kirk" and "bairn" right alongside Gaelic terms like "crag" and "whiskey"; they layered the lyrics of Northumbrian ballads upon the ancient Irish melodies of Dalriada. And throughout their history, they had few qualms about declaring war on either camp when custom or condition demanded. Just ask a Hatfield or a McCoy—get on their bad side, and they'll show you their steel.

In their pride, pluck, and pure tenacity, the border-country ancestors of the Scots-Irish provided a natural service to the tea-sipping Englishmen to the south: Their at-times prickly disposition made them natural barbed wire, a human Hadrian's Wall of sorts. For while the southern Anglicans tended to see the Scottish border people as

A nineteenth-century lesson in Scots-Irish-American studies.
These rough-and-tumble immigrants brought whiskey
know-how with them to frontier America.

half-civilized Presbyterians at best, they were still a heck of a lot better than the raging papists waiting for them up in the Highlands. And the English, with their typical colonial cunning, were happy to use the border folk to that very end. The story of the militant sect known as the Cameronians illustrates this practice perfectly. In the late 1600s, the disciples of the preacher Richard Cameron attacked state-sanctioned churches throughout the Scottish Lowlands, terrorizing clergymen who did not subscribe to their own fundamentalist brand of tent-show Calvinism. The British government initially sought to subdue the band of rebels, but quickly realized the futility of such actions. Acknowledging they could not decisively beat them, they instead decided wisely to incorporate them. In 1689, a Cameronian division was created in the British army, and those same rambunctious Lowlanders were given free rein to attack England's Catholic enemies whenever they saw fit. If you can't beat them, as the old adage goes, hire them. A similar strategy would be employed in the plantations of northern Ireland in the seventeenth century, where Scottish Lowlanders settled Ulster en masse, and, surprise, surprise, again in the wilds of Appalachia in the eighteenth and nineteenth centuries, where those same Ulster Scots once again did the dirty work for the English. James Logan, the manager of William Penn's Quaker colony, couldn't have said it any clearer:

> At the time we were apprehensive of the Northern Indians. . . . I therefore thought it might be prudent to plant a settlement of such men as those who formerly had so bravely defended Londonderry and Inniskillen as a frontier in case of any disturbance. These people . . . will also, I expect, be a leading example to others.

He got just what he was after, but also a whole lot more than he bargained for—ten years and several mountain feuds later, this same Quaker caretaker would lament that "a settlement of five families from the North of Ireland gives me more trouble than fifty of any other people." Leading examples to others these predecessors of the Hatfields and McCoys were not, but as fierce Indian fighters, they were beyond reproach—just swap out Londonderry and Enniskillen for Shenandoah and Susquehanna, and you have more or less the same devil's bargain. In exchange for land ownership and a modicum of personal and religious freedom, the Scots-Irish were willing to tame the wild edge of the American frontier. They cleared the wilderness, worshipped as they saw fit, and fought the Lenape and the Shawnee as ferociously as they once had the Pict and the Gael. Oh, and they made whiskey. A whole *lot* of whiskey. There's a simple reason bourbon calls the hills of Kentucky and Tennessee home— because the Scots-Irish who arrived in America came to settle them as well.

Although the bulk of Scots-Irish immigration would occur in the mid-eighteenth century, the fact of the matter is, both the Scots-Irish and their whiskey were in America from the very beginning. In Virginia, headrights for Irish indentured servants were granted prior to 1630, and in the year 1636 a group of 140 Protestant Irish arrived in New England. These people, known simply as "Irish" at the time, were some of the very first Scots-Irish immigrants.* They

---

* The term "Scots-Irish" was seldom used until the mid-nineteenth century, and then only by those wishing to distinguish themselves from the Irish Catholics fleeing the Potato Famine. Two things that both the Protestant Scots-Irish and the Catholic Gaelic Irish could agree on, however: The English weren't cool, and whiskey tasted delicious.

had settled first in the north of Ireland, which, for the reasons stated above, the English Crown sought to repopulate with militant Protestants, and then moved on to the early American colonies, where, if you will recall the fate of George Thorpe, there was an even greater demand for men who could handle their guns and their liquor—both qualifications the Scots-Irish had on their résumés. Between 1717 and 1775, the peak period of immigration, perhaps as many as a quarter of a million of these border people left the English colonies of Scotland and Ireland for the English colonies in America, coming at a rate of more than five thousand a year. Some stayed on the Eastern Seaboard, but many more set off for the hinterlands of Pennsylvania and Virginia, where the land they craved was still available for the taking. And American Independence—an event in which their long rifles and anti-English sentiment had played no small part—opened up even more land in Kentucky and Tennessee, frontiers that had previously been made off-limits by the British. The Scots-Irish packed their mules and wagons, headed down the famous Wilderness Trail, and poured through the previously infamous Cumberland Gap, a pass made passable by Daniel Boone himself. Cabins were built, crops were planted, and trusty old stills were fired anew. Which brings us back to the matter at hand: bourbon whiskey.

Over the course of its history and the breadth of its telling, bourbon whiskey is often imbued with semimystical characteristics. Just like baseball, rock and roll, apple pie, the fiction of Ernest Hemingway, and the cinematic splendor of *Caddyshack*, whiskey has obtained a transcendental place in our national consciousness; its substance is as much myth as fact. And while much of what would transpire in its early frontier history is open to factual debate, beyond all the extant folklore, there is a fundamental reality that can

An "illicit" nineteenth-century distilling operation.
The bourbon we know today began as backwoods whiskey.

confidently be stated. Bourbon is deemed bourbon thanks to two main factors, attributes that distinguish it from all other whiskeys: It is made primarily from corn, and it is aged in charred-oak barrels. Both techniques were tinkered with prior to the settlement of Kentucky at the end of the eighteenth century, but it was in this new frontier that they would become standard fare—not due to any divine or mystical intervention, but as the simple result of a resourceful immigrant people trying to make do in a harsh new land. It would be in the Kentucky heart of this frontier, at the turn of the nineteenth century, that distillers of Scots-Irish descent would make our nation's first true bourbon and name it as such.

First, as always, the corn. We know that corn liquor has been around in some form or another since America's proverbial get-go, but just as our first spirit was not whiskey, our first whiskey was not bourbon. In the rolling hills of Pennsylvania where many Scots-Irish initially set up camp before the opening of Kentucky, rye whiskey was being made in significant quantities during the second half of the eighteenth century. Dubbed "Monongahela" after its place of origin, this Pennsylvania rye was the de facto whiskey of the precolonial and early postcolonial era. In fact, the Whiskey Rebellion that George Washington helped quell (hold your horses, we'll get to it next chapter) just as easily could have been called the Rye Rebellion—that's what the settlers of that region were making in their pot stills, and with good reason. Rye is an Old World grain, similar to wheat in cultivation and appearance, and it thrived in the sprawling, wide-open hills of central Pennsylvania just as it had for centuries in the sprawling, wide-open hills of central Europe. With similar climates, soils, and farming methods, it was a natural fit, the perfect grain for Penn's Woods.

When the wilds of Kentucky (and Tennessee, for that matter) were opened for settlement, the ideal grain took a swift and sudden change. Your typical Scots-Irish frontiersman arriving in the new wilderness was cut off by both topography and poverty from the material availability of the urbanized seaboard; all he had to rely upon were his wits, his rifle, and the implements and seeds he could haul with him atop a mule. And the trans-Appalachian land he at last alighted upon was anything but forgiving. At best, he could clear a few acres on the steep side of a hill or at the cusp of a hollow; at worst, if it was too late in the season, he might toss a handful of seeds behind his cabin and pray for some sprouts. Faced with such harsh realities, not to mention a hotter and drier climate the farther south he

The whiskey jug would become one of many clichés
associated with the stereotypical mountaineer.

ventured, this hardscrabble mountaineer was forced out of necessity to depend upon an equally hardscrabble grain—one that could thrive on the frontier as readily as he could.

Corn.

Native Americans had been cultivating corn with minimal effort on hillsides since time immemorial. With little more than a hoe for tilling soil and a pointed stick for planting seeds, the settler could have himself a rugged little corn patch. And after just one season and a quick trip to the gristmill, he could put grits on the table and a fat sow in the barn, and, if there was any left over, which often there was, he could chop up some firewood and get out the old still.* The barley and potatoes he knew from the Old Country may have been in shorter supply, but the Scots-Irish Kentuckian never forgot how to make the liquor of his homeland(s), and he went to great lengths to ensure he never ran out of corn. As early as the spring of 1775, a Mr. William Calk noted that the pioneer population at Boonesborough, Kentucky, was "preparing for peopel to go to work to make corn." Knowing that many of these "peopel" were of Scots-Irish descent, it's hard to imagine that at least some of that maiden crop of Kentucky corn wasn't converted into one of the first barrels of true Kentucky whiskey.

Barrels, you say? As previously touched upon, the benefits of charred-oak and barrel aging were known to distillers prior to American whiskey's ascendency. "Fired" barrels were being used in the Caribbean rum industry in the late

---

* Although pioneer conditions were demanding, virgin Kentucky soil was very well suited for corn; a Kentucky farmer who planted ten acres might end up with four hundred bushels, roughly four times more than what his family and livestock would consume. With a local grain market unfriendly to sellers, it only made sense for the farmer to turn his excess corn into whiskey and send it off to be sold in distant cities where the demand was high.

eighteenth century,* and the results of barrel aging for French cognac were essentially common knowledge among commercial distillers. In a distilling manual published by Ambrose Cooper in 1757, he attributes the "Softness and Ripeness" of fine cognac to "lying in the cask," where it picked up the "Tincture of Oak." So it was no great mystery, even to early Kentucky distillers, that aging their product could increase its desirability—by 1793, advertisements appeared in Kentucky for "Old Whiskey," at a higher price than the raw, green stuff chock-full of the undesirable by-products known today as congeners.† The time spent in the charred barrel removed many of the harsher by-products through the natural contraction of the wood, and added in a touch of carbon sweetness thanks to the caramelized sugars present in the oak.‡ "Old" liquor was simply known to be better.

Spending the time and money necessary to mature the spirits, however, was another matter. Your average small-time backwoods distiller was hardly interested in letting his barrels of corn liquor gently mellow in his root cellar. He had black powder to buy, staples to acquire, and new farm implements to purchase. He needed currency ASAP, and the oak barrels brimming with liquid corn were liquid gold. With the somewhat exigent nature of frontier

---

* It's hard to say when and why barrel charring began, but based on Harrison Hall's nineteenth-century distilling manual, the practice likely started as a means of removing the rough splinters and sap bubbles from the raw oak of new barrels. After all, who wants splinter- and sap-flavored whiskey?

† Congeners include fusel oils, aldehydes, acids, furfurals, esters . . . all part of this complete breakfast.

‡ The traditional English "toast" has its roots in the seventeenth-century custom of flavoring alcohol with toasted bread—proof that the benefits of char flavoring go a long way back.

Bourbon just isn't bourbon without some quality
time spent in a charred-oak barrel. The aging process
lends whiskey much of its distinctive color and taste.

demands—Walmart was still a good two centuries away, and horse thieves and panthers didn't exactly shoot themselves—the Scots-Irish pioneer had more pressing demands than turning out an exquisite small batch bourbon. He just wanted to get paid. And what he didn't keep for his private hootenanny stash he shipped out to wherever America's parched throats beckoned, be it the Big Easy or the Big Apple. Transportation, though, was hardly quick in those days, and a simple shipment to any such city meant months aboard a mule back or riverboat. Months, as it were, of raw Kentucky corn whiskey sloshing around in a charred-oak barrel, and turning, inadvertently, into the bourbon whiskey we know today.

So when, exactly, did this phenomenon occur? That question may never be answered with exact precision; the creation story of modern Kentucky bourbon is as much myth as fact, with the former quite frequently overshadowing the latter. A firebrand preacher by the name of Elijah Craig is often credited with producing the first Kentucky bourbon aged in charred-oak barrels at a distillery established in 1789 in Fayette (later called Woodford) County. True, this besotted Baptist did produce something we would almost certainly recognize as having bourbon*esque* properties, but it is highly unlikely he was the only Kentuckian manufacturing it. Likewise, a similar creation myth can be found regarding a Mr. Jacob Spears, a pioneer and distiller from the town of Paris, Kentucky, who is said to have first used the name "bourbon" to describe the whiskey he produced there in the 1790s. Again, there is likely some truth to the story, but also a great deal of fable. Such tales are important elements of the mythology and folklore of bourbon whiskey, but they are difficult to substantiate with documentary evidence.

So, to set the record as straight as humanly possible, here's the real story of bourbon's Kentucky origin, told to

The original Bourbon Trail: The serendipitously long journey
to market was what aged bourbon in the early days.

the best of your Faithful Author's ability. Pull up a chair,
pour yourself a whiskey, and do your very best not to miss
the spittoon—bourbon's about to get promoted to the status of an official American drink.

PRIOR TO 1763, what we today know and love as the Bluegrass State belonged to the French territory of Louisiana,
and was totally verboten to early Americans. It became part
of Virginia that same year, however, which stoked the wan-
derlust of a few very early settlers, Daniel Boone chief among
them. In 1776, prompted by a certain declaration of independence, the territory played host to a flood of fresh and predominantly Scots-Irish settlers, many of whom, as we now
know, brought their stills along for the ride. By the 1780s,
corn-based whiskey was being produced throughout the
eastern and central regions of the new territory. Evan Williams? Jim Beam? The Samuels family? They all trace their

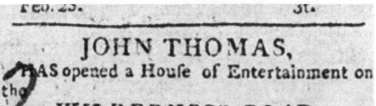

Feb. 25.   3t.

JOHN THOMAS,

HAS opened a House of Entertainment on the

WILDERNESS ROAD,

fix miles eaft of Little Rock-Caftle, at the 58 mile tree, where Travellers may be furnifhed at all times with oats at three fhillings and nine pence per bufhel, and whifkey at one fhilling and fix pence per quart, and other accommodations in proportion. He hopes from his attention to his guefts, to be favored with a portion of the public patronage.   3t†

In the late eighteenth century and early nineteenth century, "bourbon" was known simply as "whiskey," as in these Kentucky newspaper ads from the era. *Above:* announcing the opening of a "house of entertainment" offering whiskey by the quart. *Below:* Lexington merchant John Steele would like a few (thousand) of his favorite things: whiskey and bacon.

WHISKEY AND BACON
WANTED.

5000 GALLONS WHISKEY and

5000 LBS BACON to be delivered   Lexington and Frankfort, apply at
JOHN STEELE'S Hat Store.
Lexington Jan 21 1825—4-3t*

An early commercial bourbon distillery.

distilling roots to this period, with a plethora of court documents and still receipts to support them. And fortuitously, in 1785, an official county called Bourbon was established, allegedly named by Virginia assembly member James Garrard, a man of French descent who wished to demonstrate his gratitude to France's Bourbon dynasty for its assistance in the Revolution. The region encompassed a vast area of land that in its original form included some thirty-four of eastern and central Kentucky's modern counties. By 1792, when Kentucky formally became our nation's fifteenth state, this "Bourbon" region was already known locally as whiskey country. That awareness would gradually spread to the rest of the United States, traveling right alongside the exported barrels of whiskey to which it pertained. In the year 1801, whiskey and tobacco officially replaced flour as the principal export crops from the state's interior, with 50,000 gallons of the hard stuff traveling down the Ohio River and passing through the Louisville Custom House. In 1810, that number increased to 250,000 gallons, and by 1822, it exploded to 2,250,000 gallons, all bobbing in oak barrels aboard flatboats and skiffs.

And where did it all go? Well, a heck of a lot of it was destined for the terminus of the Mississippi River, New Orleans. This jewel of the delta was newly American thanks to the Louisiana Purchase, and as keen on letting the *bons temps rouler* then as it is today.[*] The Ohio River (the northern border of present-day Kentucky) fed right into the Mississippi, providing an easy aquatic shipping lane for the liquid delights of Old Bourbon County. In 1812, the residents of N'awlins received 11,000 gallons of imported whiskey; by 1816, that number had increased to 320,000 gallons, and by 1824, it stood at a whopping 570,000 gallons—all part of a whiskey boom that surely delighted backwoods distillers and Mardi Gras celebrants alike. Bourbon was literally being sold down the river, and spreading through the American South accordingly.

While much of the exported Kentucky whiskey did end up southbound on the Big Muddy, not all of it was destined for Dixie. Gradually, whiskey from Kentucky's Bourbon

---

[*] In 1818, during a lesser-known instance of Big Easy fun, a group of whiskey-drunk rivermen decided for no good reason to attack the family-friendly Gaetano's Circus midperformance. The circus folk battled valiantly, but were unable to subdue the belligerent boatmen; both their performing tiger and pet bison were clubbed to death, resulting in one gloomy day for the Cirque du Soleil.

region began traveling northeast as well, to the influential urban centers and culture capitals of the Atlantic Seaboard—not as a result of strategic marketing on the part of distillers, but rather of simple economics. With most Western farmers able to produce more corn than they needed, there wasn't much of a local market for the grain. And paying to haul bulky bushels of corn over the Appalachians to the needy grain markets of the East? Also a losing economic venture. But corn *whiskey* on the other hand . . . well, with a horse able to carry six times as much corn in liquid form as it could otherwise, and with shipping on the Ohio River still exceptionally cheap, sending excess grain eastward in the form of alcohol, by land or water, made far more sense. And so, in addition to the Southern market at the end of the Mississippi, the frontier distiller found himself with a second market in the metropolises of the East. In the first decades of the nineteenth century, barrels of Kentucky corn whiskey began appearing in the taverns and inns of America's northeastern capitals, where it quickly gained a reputation—even among the most urbane of Yankees—for its palatability and smoothness. The following passage from an 1818 treatise on distillation, published in Philadelphia by the distiller Harrison Hall, is only lacking a bow when it comes to wrapping up what was happening to bourbon, and America, at that time:

> *The rapidity of improvements in the western parts of the United States, is a matter of some consideration to the distillers of the Atlantic States. They have already made considerable progress in the art of distillation, and the vast quantities of grain which are produced by their fertile lands, beyond the necessary consumption, cannot be so well disposed of in any way as in pork and whiskey.*

Here we already find Tennessee and Kentucky whiskey in our sea ports, and it is generally preferred to that made nearer home; this by the way, is a powerful argument against the common prejudice against using corn, and the western whiskey is chiefly made of that grain. . . . As they depend upon the rise of the rivers to send their whiskey to market, it acquires some age: this also, and the motion of travelling, has considerable effect in improving it.

With little more than a few run-on sentences, Mr. Hall described the transformation of bourbon from a raw by-product of Scots-Irish pioneering to a mature regional beverage enjoyed well beyond its original frontier.

One omission is notable, however: Harrison Hall makes no mention of "Bourbon" in his description, nor does he designate aged corn whiskey as such. Just when did the moniker come about? Once again, it's difficult to say with any precision. The very first printed advertisement for "BOURBON WHISKEY" appears in the *Western Citizen* in 1821, at the behest of the Kentucky firm of Stout and Adams, although this very early mention is something of an anomaly, and likely more geographic in connotation than qualitative—the generic term of "whiskey" appeared far more often in the two decades that followed. By the 1840s, however, whiskey barrels from Kentucky's original Old Bourbon County were being labeled precisely that way.* Just as scotch comes from

---

* "Old" applies to the former borders of the original Bourbon County, but was commonly used in the Scots-Irish Upland South to connote something both beloved and marked by tradition—think "Old Hickory," "My Old Kentucky Home," and of course those good *old* Duke boys, never meanin' no harm. The word "Old" will play a role in bourbon naming for the totality of its history, from Old Forester to Old Crow.

1847
ROBBERTSON'S
GENUINE
BOURBON
CORDIAL.
HARRISON C° KENTUCKY.

By the 1840s, the name "bourbon" finally caught on, used
to describe the aged corn whiskey that came from Kentucky.

Scotland, and "Old Monongahela" rye once came from that
part of Pennsylvania, Kentucky whiskey took on the name of
its original place of origin, the massive swath of hill country
that constituted the earliest borders of Bourbon County. A
price listing from Maysville in 1848 states that "Old Bourbon is worth 37½ @ 1.00 according to age," and a newspaper advert from 1852 announces the availability of "Old
Bourbon" from "2 to 4 years old for sale."

Not long after, the "Old" was dropped, and that oak-
aged Kentucky corn whiskey became known simply as bourbon. In 1854, Thomas Eales of Paris, Kentucky, announced
that he had for sale "150 barrels of superior copper distilled
Bourbon whiskey, from one to six years old." Four years

after that, the Maysville company of R. H. Newell shilled for "1000 Barrels Bourbon Whiskey, 1 to 4 years old." And it wasn't just the Bluegrass State calling it bourbon and savoring its flavor—in 1861, Prince Napoleon, paying a visit to the military camps at Staten Island from France, sampled a glass of bourbon given to him by a private and wryly remarked, "I did not think I would like anything with that name so well." This is all evidence that "bourbon" was definitely part of the colloquial vocabulary by the middle of the nineteenth century, and by the outbreak of the Civil War, whiskey called "bourbon," distilled primarily by the Kentucky descendants of Scots-Irish pioneers, was being shipped in large quantities to destinations both north and south, to be enjoyed on the two increasingly divergent sides of the Mason-Dixon.

And our young and feisty American Spirit, with its roots in rebellion and in the crucible of the frontier, is about to have its allegiances tested in the sorest of fashions.

4
Bourbon's Rebellious Phase

UNHOLY SCREAMS, BLOOD-SPATTERED aprons, saw-wielding doctors with liquor-laced breath—the common perceptions of Civil War–era medicine are not way off the mark, but they're not entirely accurate, either. True, battlefield surgery was a gory affair, with limbs being lopped and left in a pile. But contrary to popular belief, the vast majority of such operations occurred while the patient was mercifully anesthetized with ether or chloroform. Yes, whiskey was used medicinally as a sedative, liberally at that, by both doctors and patients alike. But while the familiar "take a swig and bite the bullet" scenario popularized in cinema and literature surely did occur in the direst of circumstances, it was by no means standard fare. Rather than dig up some such anecdote and burnish it with the sensational, we're going to begin bourbon's Civil War chapter with an account far less clichéd and far more revealing.

So let us commence not with some slurring surgeon or commissary quack, but with a distinguished and highly educated doctor by the name of John H. Brinton, who served in the Union army as a commissioned brigade surgeon between 1861 and 1865. A trusted friend to General Grant, and the right-hand man to the surgeon general at a time when the position demanded both surgery and generalship, Dr. Brinton took part in one of the greatest periods of medical advancement on record. And while this sudden surge in medical innovation was due primarily to the hideous textbook that the maimed flesh of countless soldiers provided, it was also made possible thanks to a certain corn-based and uniquely American form of alcohol that, by the first report of cannon fire upon Fort Sumter, had secured its place as the common spirit of North and South alike—a fact that an amusing although cringe-worthy anecdote involving the good Dr. Brinton will demonstrate quite nicely.

It was not long into the service of John Brinton that, among the mounds of severed legs and reams of ruined faces, he came to recognize the vast educational potential such injuries could provide for the many medical schools back east. From his own days as a medical student at the University of Philadelphia and later Thomas Jefferson University, he knew firsthand the invaluable learning tools that cadavers and anatomical specimens inherently provided—the types of trauma witnessed in wartime were rare under peacetime conditions, and as such, difficult to teach or study. The bullet-smashed bones and the shrapnel-riddled organs stacked outside Union surgery tents were desperately needed to instruct future generations of doctors in just how horrific the horrors of war could be. So when the surgeon general requested specimens for the newly formed Army Medical Museum in the nation's capital, John H. Brinton was happy to oblige. Except for one small problem: The battlefields and corps hospitals where such specimens could be found were hundreds of miles from Washington D.C. Traversing that distance required a long ride in the bed of a sweltering railcar—hardly the ideal conditions for transporting flesh and bone that was usually rotting to begin with. What they needed was a preservative, and one

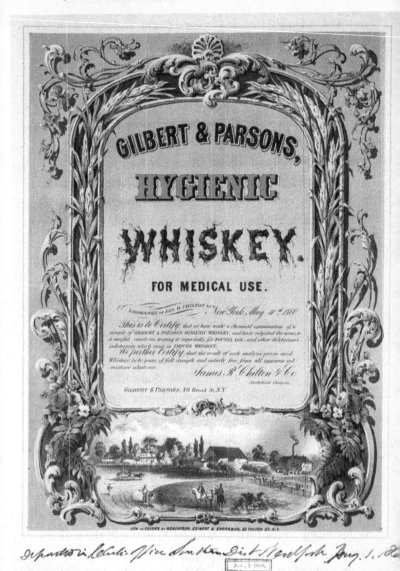

Just what the doctor ordered: Whiskey and the medical industry go way back.
This ad for "hygienic whiskey for medical use" is dated to 1860; the product
would soon find its way to Civil War operating rooms—when it wasn't being
siphoned off for private consumption.

available in copious wartime quantities at that. What they needed was a healthy dose of bourbon whiskey.

Thanks to the strict alcohol policies of the provost general, they found it. Since the commencement of the war, stringent regulations had been placed on the production, sale, and distribution of alcohol within the Union. Given its importance in battlefield medicine, its crucial role in the manufacture of munitions, and its timeless utility as a universal currency, alcohol became a precious and highly restricted commodity. This quite naturally encouraged a black market for such spirituous goods, and with Kentucky officially part of the Union, and at least the eastern portion of Tennessee similarly inclined, much of the contraband whiskey in the capital was pouring in from the traditional distilleries of America's bourbon heartland. All of which, once confiscated by the government, provided the perfect medical preservative for Dr. John H. Brinton's battlefield specimens. And the generous provost general was delighted to supply for posterity's sake as much of the whiskey as the good doctor needed.

But even that liberal allotment proved to be curiously insufficient. For the baffled battlefield doctors began to notice that the barrels of whiskey preservative being sent from the museum were surprisingly light upon their arrival at camp. Any distiller worth his salt knows of the "angel's share," that magical portion of whiskey claimed from the cask by the scientific cherubim of evaporation, but such phenomena took years to transpire, and generally claimed only a small percentage— these barrels were showing up after only a few days' voyage less than half full. No, the museum's whiskey barrels were most definitely leaking, and upon hearing reports of their missing contents, a culprit less angelic and far more corporeal immediately came to John Brinton's mind. To test his hypothesis, he inspected one of the museum's choicest whiskey barrels prior to shipping off, and slipped in a small amount of tartar emetic—an incredibly potent substance used by doctors of that era to induce fierce bouts of projectile vomiting.

John H. Brinton never was able to single out any one source of the "leak," but he did follow the particular rail line that his specially treated whiskey barrel had taken, and as a doctor, took careful note of the large number of military officers and railroad men who had called in sick along the way, complaining of a common and curiously vague stomach ailment. Additionally, he also noticed that shortly thereafter, the mysterious leaking whiskey phenomenon of the museum's barrels ceased altogether. The kegs from the capital began arriving in front of the military camp doctors just as they had been sent: untainted, untampered with, and filled to the brim with bourbon.

The story of Dr. Brinton's bourbon is hardly unique or exceptional in its portrayal of whiskey during the Civil War—such tales abound in the historical documents of the era. The spirit played a surprisingly declarative role in our national conflict, with the respective tides and fortunes of each side reflecting almost eerily in the status and availability at any one moment of their cherished American drink. To gain even a small sense of bourbon's Civil War ubiquity, one need only rattle off a quick roll call of the very men who captained it, beginning with the highest echelons of power. Abraham Lincoln—president of the Union—was a native-born Kentuckian, the son of a part-time distiller, who once applied for an Illinois liquor license to run a tavern and sell Kentucky whiskey. Jefferson Davis, his Confederate counterpart, was also a son of the Bluegrass State, and according to record, a longtime aficionado of the liquid delights of his homeland. General Ulysses S. Grant was a legendary bourbon drinker, at times problematically so, although his alleged passion for Old Crow never lessened

Abraham Lincoln's
Liquor License and Bond

Ordered that William F. Berry in the name of Berry and Lincoln have license to keep a tavern in New Salem to continue 12 months from this date and that they pay one dollar in addition to six dollars heretofore paid as for treasury receipt, and that they be allowed the following rates viz;

French Brandy per ½ pint	25	Breakfast dinner or Supper	25		
Peach	18¾	Lodging for night	12½		
Apple	12	House per night	25		
Holland Gin	18¾	Single feed	12½		
Domestic	12½	Breakfast dinner or }			
Wine	25	Supper for Stage passengers }	37½		
Rum	18¾				
Whiskey	12½				

Who gave bond as required by law

FACSIMILE OF TAVERN LICENSE ISSUED TO BERRY AND LINCOLN.
Certified by Chas. E. Oppel, Clerk, Sangamon County Court, Springfield, Ill. Date April 25, 1908

Know all men by there presents:

We, William F. Berry, Abraham Lincoln and John Bowling Green, are held and firmly bound unto the County Commissioners of Sangamon County in the full sum of three hundred dollars, to which payment well and truly to be made we bind ourselves, our heirs, executors and administrators firmly by these presents, sealed with our seal and dated this 6th day of March, A.D. 1833. Now the condition of this obligation is such that, whereas the said Berry and Lincoln has obtained a license from the County Commissioners' Court to keep a tavern in the Town of New Salem to continue one year. Now if the said Berry and Lincoln shall be of good behavior and observe all the laws of this State relative to tavern keepers then this obligation to be void or otherwise remain in full force.

ABRAHAM LINCOLN, [Seal]
WILLIAM F. BERRY, [Seal]
BOWLING GREEN, [Seal]

Facsimile of bond given by Abraham Lincoln, William F. Berry and John Bowling Green binding themselves in a penalty of $300 not to sell whiskey to negroes, Indians or children, i.e. to obey the liquor laws of the State.

IT IS UPON RECORD that the firm of "Berry & Lincoln" of New Salem, Ill. employed Daniel Greene, who states, "While I was there, they had nothing for sale but liquors... I used to sell whiskey over the counter at 6 cents a glass." See Norman Hapgood's "Lincoln, the Man of the People" date 1899 page 37; Also Col. Lamon's "Life of Lincoln" pages 137, 138. MESSRS. BERRY & LINCOLN afterwards purchased the village tavern owned by Jas. Rutledge; also another "grocery." Thus they had three "places" where brandy, whiskey, wine and rum were sold daily. The word "grocery" always meant, in those days, a store where liquor was sold. In Ida Tarbell's "Life of Lincoln" Vol. I, page 94, "Each of the three groceries which Berry & Lincoln acquired had the usual supply of liquors.

A souvenir facsimile of Abe Lincoln's liquor license, acquired when he opened a tavern in New Salem, Illinois, in 1833.

his battlefield prowess. His rival, General Robert E. Lee, was a lover of fine bourbon whiskey as well, although he abstained from liquor whenever possible; he would gracefully remark, "I like whiskey. I always did, and that is why I never drink it." The North's famous Fighting Joe Hooker had no such reservations. Also a whiskey man, Hooker enjoyed his drink, if the stories are to be believed, almost as much as he did his ladies, and his headquarters were often cited as being equal parts saloon and brothel. In fact, one of the few major generals, North or South, who vehemently spoke out against whiskey in all forms was George B. McClellan. His review of court-martial cases involving intoxication are a veritable diatribe against the presence of alcohol in the ranks, with him stating at one point that total abstinence from liquor "would be worth 50,000 men to the armies of the United States." Whether such abstinence had any salutary effect on his own career is difficult to say. But by the war's end, McClellan's gross incompetence had cost him his command, and Lincoln was offering only half in jest to buy his other generals a case of Grant's preferred bourbon, in the hope it might inspire similar victories. And through all of this turmoil, tumult, and strife, the fledgling bourbon industry of a still relatively young nation would struggle to keep from being rent asunder. The eventual prevalence of the North and the surrender of the South, while not dictated by whiskey, would be foretold in bourbon barrels long before the guns of the latter finally lost their bark at Appomattox. And while painful years of Reconstruction would be required to repair the damage done to both nation and libation, the American Spirit that prevailed would prove stronger, more unified, and more clearly entrenched than the one a divided people had once so bloodily cleaved.

To find the seeds of the four-year conflict that very nearly split America in twain, we must go back to its founding, to when they were first sown by none other than bourbon's controversial father, Captain George Thorpe. Those very first "plantations" in the Virginia Tidewater, of which George's Berkeley plantation was among the more prominent, became dependent upon an agrarian monoculture that focused on a single cash crop: tobacco. George's tremendous initial success in getting the Virginia Company's tobacco leaves out the door and back to European markets would set the stage for a new form of plantation agriculture unique to the American South. Initially, the region's tobacco fields were tended by indentured servants and low-paid laborers, a fair portion of whom were land-hungry Scots-Irish struggling to pay off their debts and pining for the frontier. When indentured servitude proved to be less profitable than the lords of the manors had hoped, they took their cue from the Spanish, who had been running a Caribbean plantation economy of their own for more than a century, and began importing human chattel in the form of African slaves.

Jamestown was using slave labor as early as 1619, although the first legally recognized slave would not appear in America until 1654. In the early eighteenth century, with indentured servitude petering out; prices on labor-intensive plantation crops like rice, indigo, and tobacco booming; and our previously mentioned glut of colonial rum available as African currency, slavery became a fixed institution in the Southern colonies—the fortunes of their most prominent citizens depended upon it, many of our own Founding Fathers among them. Following the Revolution, this dependence on slavery became even more solidified; while plantation-free Northern states officially abandoned whatever vestiges lingered of the "peculiar institution," the Southern states passed laws to ensure the survival of their own slave-based economy.

With Eli Whitney's 1793 invention of the cotton gin, a machine that rendered a previously unruly crop astronomically profitable, the course of the core Southern states became fixed, much to the detriment of the millions of men and women forced to labor under subhuman conditions for the sake of the crop's cultivation and manufacture. As Frederick Douglass, himself a former slave and a leading abolitionist of the day, would cry out to the nation, "The same spirits which make a white man drunk make a black man drunk too. Indeed, in this I can find proof of my identity with the family of man."

All of which created a fair amount of tension in Washington, but none of which was nation-ruining, prior to 1861. Before that fateful year, a sort of uneasy truce existed between the twin halves of our callow young country—a northern half that was increasingly urban, manufacturing-based, and immigrant-inclined, and a southern half, capable of maintaining its aristocratic traditions, economic independence, and political stature so long as slavery persisted. This equilibrium was tenuous but sustainable on the condition that borders remained static. But the expansion into newly opened western territories and the addition of new states threw the fragile balance of power way off-kilter. Each new star sewn onto the flag had all the ominous potential of a discarded cigarette butt, flicked carelessly into the powder keg of hostility that existed between North and South.

Wedged uncomfortably between the two behemoths was a sassy border state called Kentucky, one that allowed slavery, but whose geography, climate, and culture engendered considerable ambivalence on the matter. With the 1860 election of Republican Abraham Lincoln—a man of Kentucky stock known to be against slavery's expansion—the tipping point for Southern secession was finally reached. Lines were drawn, shots were fired, and the Commonwealth of Kentucky, with its crucial border position, easy access to the Mississippi River, and yes, burgeoning bourbon industry, found itself forced to choose sides. Honest Abe knew exactly how pivotal that decision would be, declaring, "I hope to have God on my side, but I must have Kentucky."

Jefferson Davis, the emerging president of the Confederacy, was also a native-born Kentuckian, and he too coveted the commonwealth with equal vehemence, recognizing the cost of losing the strategic support of his Old Kentucky Home. And yet again, the whiskey drinkers of what once had been a wild frontier found themselves a much-coveted buffer between two warring factions. Not Saxon and Celt, not Catholic and Protestant, not even Colonial and Indian, but instead the two halves of some suddenly dis-United States . . . and the Commonwealth of Kentucky had a tough decision to make.

On September 4, 1861, General Leonidas Polk made the ill-advised decision to tromp Confederate boots upon their beloved Bluegrass. When the Confederacy invaded, the Kentucky General Assembly, previously staunch in its neutrality, felt no other option than to ask the Union for help . . . and in doing so, joined the effort to preserve it. A brigadier general by the name of Ulysses S. Grant—an untested officer known more for his bouts of solitary bourbon drinking at lonely frontier outposts than for martial might—stormed into Kentucky from Illinois, drove out the Rebels, and managed to secure invaluable access to the mighty Mississippi, as well as the crucial New Orleans and Ohio railroads. In achieving command of the region's primary shipping lanes, he gained control of the region's primary products of export, and secured the crucial bourbon leg of the nation's whiskey pipeline.

While the whiskey well ran dry for the freshly blockaded South, the North had the traditional rye distilleries of western Pennsylvania and Maryland in its pocket, the newer and more industrial-minded distilleries of upstate New York and southwest Ohio in its corner, and, at last, the traditional bourbon heartland of Kentucky unambiguously on its side. The Southern spigot in the bourbon barrel was plugged; the North controlled the Mississippi, along with every crate and barrel that went down it. And although production challenges would certainly hamper the Kentucky distilleries—as many as one hundred thousand young men of prime corn-harvesting and whiskey-distilling age were serving in the Union army, while some thirty thousand young Kentuckians had defected to the Confederacy—what they did manage to pump out of their stills during wartime had the Union army as its biggest and most reliable buyer. As Captain Thomas H. Parker of the 51st Pennsylvania Infantry would note upon entering Lexington, "Pies, soft bread, cheese, and last but not least, canteens full of 'old Bourbon,' were the articles most sought, especially the whiskey."

Since when did Yankees like whiskey so much? Alas, despite whiskey's modern connotations of jug-toting Rebels and julep-tossing Faulkners, the liquor's production and enjoyment have never been the sole province of the South. In fact, whiskey's first "Rebel Yell" was not uttered on any mid-bellum Southern battlefield, but in western Pennsylvania in 1794, when small farmers and distillers rose up as one defiant body against U.S. marshals sent in to collect a highly unpopular excise tax on grain spirits, creating their own flag and declaring regional independence along the way. This decidedly Northern Whiskey Rebellion against the central govern-

A cause worth fighting for: The Whiskey Rebellion predated
Southern secession by almost seventy-five years.

ment predated the South's insurrection by more than half a
century, and created enough of a stir to get President Washington back on his white horse to lead thirteen thousand
troops on a march toward Pittsburgh to calm things down.

Granted, the Whiskey Rebellion resulted in only half a
dozen fatalities, making it roughly one hundred thousand
times less deadly than the War of Southern Secession that
followed, but it still serves as a poignant reminder that whiskey in the mid-nineteenth century was truly a pan-American
drink, enjoyed by Northerners and Southerners alike, and
hardly a regional tipple to be downed exclusively by white-
suited gentlemen who looked like Colonel Sanders and spoke
like Foghorn Leghorn.

Where's the proof? By 1840, more than half of our
nation's grain spirits came from the unambiguously Northern states of Ohio, New York, and Pennsylvania; by 1850,
Pennsylvania had more distilleries than any other state in
the Union, although the growing industrial distilleries of
Ohio and New York produced more alcohol by volume.
Kentucky was up there, too, though not quite yet in the top
three. What the bourbon-producing border state lacked at

that time in quantity, however, it more than made up for in quality, as illustrated by the remembrance of one Lieuten-ant Colonel Isaac Stewart, who served under General Grant during Union efforts to gain control of the Mississippi River:

> I think it was on the night of February 23, '63, down at Vicksburg. We were all pretty tired and sat in the cabin of the river steamer, the Magnolia, waiting for the morning. My stateroom was next to the General's [Grant's], and I was thinking of turning in when the General said to McPherson: "See here, before we go to bed let us have a nightcap. Stewart has got some prime Old Crow whiskey around here somewhere." I went to my stateroom and brought out the bottle. The General filled a goblet—not a little one, but a good big goblet—to the brim with that Old Crow whiskey, and he tossed it off.[*]

It only stands to reason that the man soon to control one of the largest armies ever assembled in the history of the world would drink nothing but the best, and in 1863, the fin-est was a goblet full of good barrel-aged Kentucky bourbon. As for the historians who dispute claims of Grant's penchant for bourbon—and there are a fair number—they should at least consider the words of someone who was in a darn good position to know, William Tecumseh Sherman, who famously said of Grant: "I know him well. He stood by me when I was

---

[*] Interesting side note: As we shall soon see, Old Crow bourbon was created by Scottish immigrant James C. Crow, a distiller who settled near Woodford County, Kentucky, in the 1820s and invented the sour mash process used by many of the top bourbon brands today . . . proof that despite their thrifty reputation, when it comes to whiskey, the Scots just keep on giving.

crazy, and I stood by him when he was drunk; and now, sir, we stand by each other always." It is often remarked that it takes one to know one, and sure enough, as declared in his own memoirs, General Sherman was as crazy for bourbon as he was, well, nuts in general—he carried a flask of good whiskey in his saddlebag, right beside his maps and cigars, all during his hellacious campaign through Georgia, all throughout his infamous March to the Sea, taking generous puffs and swigs as he saw fit.

The enlisted man, however, was not quite so fortunate as his commanding Union officers when it came time to tipple. Unlike his medal-festooned superiors, his imbibing was more carefully restricted, and he seldom had good bourbon within easy reach. But the poor buck private did not go entirely without drink—whiskey was available, and generally acquired in one of two ways. The first was legitimate, either through officer-sanctioned rations or doctor-approved pre-scriptions. The second way was far less so, and generally entailed buying black market booze smuggled into camp, or, if he was deep in Rebel territory, having the good fortune to stumble upon a Confederate still.

As for whiskey acquired legitimately, the same U.S. Army liquor rations that had once won George Washington the loyalty of his troops were officially abolished in 1830, though field commanders were still allowed the loophole of distributing small quantities of commissary whiskey to their men, particularly as a reward for good service[*] or as a buffer against the cold. A young fifer of the 1st Massachu-

---

[*] At Antietam Creek, a certain General Burnside, famous for his face-flanking whiskers, ordered the 51st New York and 51st Pennsylvania regiments to take control of one particularly contested bridge. The men agreed to do so . . . in exchange for one barrel of whiskey, which they drank triumphantly the next day.

A Civil War poker night just wasn't complete
without a bottle of whiskey on hand.

setts Infantry received his first taste of whiskey during a particularly dark and chillsome morn, and although hesitant at first, he found great comfort in that ante meridiem swig, and noted that on every occasion thereafter, "when the commanding officer gave out whiskey I yielded to his better judgment."

On the medical front, whiskey was widely available to those for whom it was deemed necessary, with prescriptions written for everything from flesh wounds to gonorrhea. While medicinal whiskey was seldom used as a general anesthetic, it was frequently used as an analgesic and prescribed to soldiers in need of its comfort and balm. Naturally, this sanctioned conduit for whiskey distribution created the potential for abuse, and as the clever Dr. Brinton learned earlier in this chapter, "medical" whiskey often ended up in the bellies of otherwise healthy men. One particularly brazen and semiliterate hospital worker from Vermont used his ambulatory position to smuggle in whiskey from back home and sell it to soldiers, telling his own son in a letter "when yo Send it Direct it to Doctor Sawin Just as yo have the rest," and further claiming that the whiskey would "bring me good too hundred dollars the minet I get it." Unfortunately for this enterprising capitalist, his luck would prove even worse than his spelling—before his tour of duty was complete, he fell headfirst off a hospital boat and drowned. Unscrupulous medics aside, however, many a scarred or shell-shocked soldier found welcome relief in a dose of good whiskey, be it at the behest of a compassionate officer or at that of a caring doctor . . . and if the soldier was lucky, that healing bottle would hold not the sterile grain spirit of one of the North's burgeoning industrial alcohol distilleries, but the savory salve of genuine, good old-fashioned, oak-aged bourbon.

Now for the somewhat less than legitimate means for

procuring whiskey, methods that ceaselessly occupied Union soldiers, and relentlessly irked their commanding officers. Ordinarily, a general would look the other way when some of his weary men took a casual nip. But when the whiskey ran too freely, the brass had good reason to crack down, and the first folks they looked to punish were the men known as "sutlers." Traveling salesmen of sorts, the sutlers of the Civil War served as commercial intermediaries between the encamped soldiers and the outside world, selling staples that were otherwise hard to find. One offering that they often snuck in against military orders and hid in their tents was whiskey. A young Irish immigrant by the name of William Wallace marched with the 1st Wisconsin Regiment during the Virginia Campaign, and wrote of one such incident in a letter to his family:

> After breakfast some of the boys smelled some whiskey in the sutlers tent belonging to the Indiana 27th, some got drunk. By and by Colonel Ruger heard it, when he sent a squad of men to the aforesaid tent and arrested the 3 sutlers and placed them under guard and immediately confiscated his whole property, 4 fine horses, and 4 mules and 2 wagons and all of his stock of goods, as he was violating the army regulations in selling licquers to the soldiers.

Colonel Ruger's strict whiskey policy may seem draconian, but it was not without good reason. The illicit alcohol being scooped up by soldiers not only endangered them on the battlefield, it also could literally stop them dead in their tracks—while passing through Maryland on their way to meet the enemy, the regiment shot a Confederate sympathizer through the head for trying to poison a camp well with arsenic, and immediately after that placed

SEARCHING FOR WHISKEY

"Searching for Whiskey": a full-time job
for Union and Confederate troops alike.

two other men under guard, charged with "selling butter
and vegetables and whiskey full of poison." One can only
surmise that whatever the locals slipped into the whiskey
was considerably more lethal than Dr. John H. Brinton's
tartar emetic.

And the other illegitimate scenario? Stumbling upon a
hidden stock of Confederate whiskey on Southern soil. This
could mean discovering a store of liquor at a grocery or private home, but given the South's own whiskey woes to be
discussed shortly, uncovering pre-blockade packaged whiskey became increasingly unlikely as the war progressed.
The more frequent occurrence was the revelation of a clan-

destine still being used to make liquor on the sly. Such stills could often be found in close vicinity to mills, where the raw grain was ground into distilling-friendly grist. On a rainy day not long after detaining the men for selling poisoned whiskey to the Union troops, William Wallace and company "commandeered" a barrel of far-superior whiskey at a mill outside of Honeyville, Virginia. According to Wallace, "Every man filled his canteen and made to drink on the spot and did not do us a bit of harm, for it was still raining like fury." We can assume the aforementioned Colonel Ruger was kept blissfully in the dark about the whole affair.

Similar instances of whiskey commandeering would occur throughout the course of the war, culminating in the Union's tapping of the biggest Southern whiskey barrel of all: New Orleans. When Northern troops moved into the French Quarter in May of 1862, they discovered that Bourbon Street, although named after the French dynasty, did not shy away from the second connotation of its title—the whiskey flowed like water, funneled downriver via the Mighty Mississippi and concentrated for both enjoyment and sale in one of the world's most festive cities. And those Union troops, as even a quick skim over the court-martial records of that campaign will show, partied their federal asses off accordingly. The very best court-martials come by way of the famous Irish brigade known as the Connecticut "Fighting Ninth" Volunteer Infantry, the soldiers of which proved to be as heroic at whiskey drinking as they were in battle. So what did these Mardi Gras–worthy offenses entail? What follows is a brief and pretty darn amusing summation of their New Orleans exploits:

A private named Peter Flanagan was accused of being

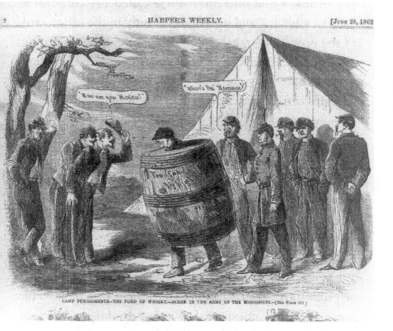

Some Civil War officers got creative when it came to
punishing the rampant drunkenness among the ranks.

drunk twice on their march into the Big Easy, in addition to cursing his captain and seizing him by the whiskers. Another private by the name of Henry Connell
faced similar charges, and had to have his trial delayed
for a week because he was still too drunk to understand
the proceedings. Messieurs Dennis Gregg and John
McClune broke into the house of a private citizen, cursed
the home owner when he denied them whiskey, and then
said they wanted "to piss, in front of [his] wife." Patrick
Gray was arrested drunk while wearing civilian clothes,
claiming that he'd been "on a three day spree and [his]
uniform was at the house of a woman on Phillippa
Street." Another Patrick, but with the surname Conan,

got drunk while on sentry duty, called his corporal a "son of a bitch," and urinated defiantly in the office yard of the provost marshal. The private John Heffernan? He also became drunk on duty, and commenced uttering "treasonable and seditious" language while attacking a superior officer with an iron bar. An intoxicated Thomas Cummings told his lieutenant he'd "put a bullet in [his] head," an inebriated John S. Murphy fired a musket in Lafayette Square and "pissed himself," and a captain by the name of Terrence Sheridan tried to have sex with a stewardess aboard a steamship called the *Iberville*, frightened her so badly she hid, and then commenced to stumble about "not staggering drunk, but still able to walk."

Model soldierly behavior? Probably not, but given the hell that surrounded them, military mischief on the part of soldiers is hardly unexpected. Whiskey drinking served as a release of sorts, whether sanctioned or not, and the temporary escape it provided from the pressures of war and the misery of camp conditions was exploited by all ranks and classes, from a battle-harried top general named Ulysses S. Grant, on down to that low-ranking fifer shivering in the snow during revelry at four in the morning. And thanks to the strategic, economic, and industrial advantages that the Northern states had on their side from the war's onset, their crucial bourbon supply was kept flowing throughout the course of the conflict. Advertisements would continue to appear in *Harper's Weekly* offering thirsty New Yorkers bourbon whiskey direct from Kentucky "in barrels, half-barrels, and cases," and at the bar of the Willard Hotel in our nation's capital, the "universal habit" of ordering bourbon mint juleps would go on unabated, made possible by an unending current of political discourse, and a steady stream of whiskey from a crucial border state.

The whiskey success that the Union secured early in the war came at the expense of the Confederates' own local supply. With the implementation of General Winfield Scott's "Anaconda Plan" to blockade the Confederacy's Atlantic and Gulf Coast ports, the Union effectively severed the South's economic ties to the outside world. With the exception of a very limited amount of smuggling and blockade-running, the Confederate states were sealed off from the foreign markets that bought their tobacco and cotton, and in return supplied their capital and manufactured goods. When Kentucky's General Assembly made the fateful decision to raise the Stars and Stripes rather than the Stars and Bars over Frankfort, their bourbon whiskey became a "foreign" product for the South, subject to the same embargo that prevented medicine, muskets, money, and manpower from entering the Confederacy and empowering their military effort. The Southern army and society were both left with a serious shortage of alcohol. And as a consequence, your average Confederate was considerably less whiskey-prone than popular conceptions of jug-hugging Rebels might suggest. Not to say whiskey wasn't aggressively sought by soldier and commander alike—it often was, for reasons that ranged from medical to purely social, and black market liquor thrived on that demand. But for most Confederates, bourbon was as coveted and yet unattainable as a potshot at Lincoln.

Not much historical digging is required to find convincing examples of Southern temperance during the war effort. We can start right at the top with General Robert E. Lee. Although admittedly fond of whiskey, he took great care to avoid it in any substantial quantity, as he was well aware of the toll overindulgence could have on a military man's career. In a letter to his son, recently inducted into martial life, Lee would write:

*I hope you will always be distinguished for your avoidance
of the "universal balm," whiskey, and every immorality.
Nor need you fear to be ruled out of the society that
indulges in it, for you will acquire their esteem and
respect, as all venerate if they do not practice virtue. I am
sorry to say that there is a great proclivity for spirit in the
army field. It seems to be considered a substitute for every
luxury. The great body may not carry it to excess, but
many pursue it to their ruin.*

As far as generals go, Lee may have been the most prominent teetotaler, but he was hardly alone in his abstemious
ways. General Braxton Bragg, as fierce a proponent of temperance as he was of states' rights, prohibited the sale of
alcohol within five miles of his troops in Pensacola, declaring
most vociferously, "We have lost more valuable lives at the
hands of the whiskey sellers than by the balls of our enemies." Exaggeration, most definitely, but a sentiment
reflected in the orders of Thomas Jonathan Jackson, aka
"Stonewall," who took a similar position when it came to
whiskey. Although like his partner-in-secessionism Robert E.
Lee, he admitted to a considerable predilection for whiskey,
he was known to avoid it on most occasions, even telling one
soldier left to guard a store of whiskey, "I fear that liquor
more than General Pope's Army," shortly before ordering it
destroyed. Jackson did, however, find at least two occasions
when whiskey suited him: once, when a bottle of fine aged
liquor was gifted upon him in the Shenandoah Valley, leading him to become "incipiently tight," and again upon his
fatal wounding at Chancellorsville—both whiskey and mor-
phine were administered to him as he lay dying.

Although many Confederate officers would follow the
lead of Generals Lee and Jackson, and concur with General

Custer's last keg stand: A young George Armstrong (front right)
pregames with his fellow soldiers.

Bragg that whiskey held the potential to cause "demoraliza-
tion, disease, and death," many others did not. Some, like
General Reuben Davis, personally sent up barrels of "Oh-be-
joyful" to their camps, a small reprieve from battle for all the
"old soakers" craving a drink. Others, like one resourceful
Georgia colonel, even set up a still and made their own. But
a common perception among the average Confederate foot
soldiers was that real whiskey—particularly smuggled
bourbon—was the domain of privileged officers, men who,
according to the October 25, 1862, diary entry of one anony-
mous Louisiana soldier, were "better able to command a

bottle of whiskey than anything else." At times, this state of affairs caused considerable resentment, as officers did not face the same prohibition against alcohol as the lay soldier did, and could purchase it, when available, at their own discretion. True, some low-ranking soldiers actively chose to practice the South's own version of the temperance movement, even equating drinking with Northern collusion. But for a far larger body of Confederate soldiers, warring against the Union was an understandably throat-parching endeavor, and getting their hands on whiskey was a full-time job . . . or at the very least, a damn-serious hobby.

"Western whiskey," as Kentucky bourbon was still called at that time, was exceedingly rare, if not virtually unobtainable, thanks to the Union's stranglehold blockade. Cornfields, upon which the mash bills of Southern whiskey were utterly dependent, were essentially untended, with the little corn that was harvested going directly toward feeding the military and civilian populations. And Southern whiskey stills, if not disassembled and scrapped for their much-needed copper, had nothing to cook up and nobody to work them—dire straits, indeed. For a Confederate soldier to wet his whistle with wartime whiskey, he would need to resort to some pretty creative measures, and display considerably more resourcefulness than his Northern counterpart, for whom good whiskey—even bourbon—was scarce but hardly unavailable.

When it came to whiskey, one option that the Southern combatant did have in common with those serving with the Union was a "medicinal prescription." Thanks to a severe shortage of medical supplies, the South was even more reliant than the North on liquor, as it was often a substitute for the proper medicines no longer available under the blockade. When quinine ran out, the Rebels relied on a concoction called "old indig"—whiskey mixed with dried dogwood bark—to relieve malaria's symptoms. And when ether or chloroform proved unavailable for surgery, whiskey served as a poor but passable substitute. For this reason, Confederates were generally more conscious than Union troops of the necessity of maintaining their meager whiskey supplies. Rufus Peck, a Confederate soldier of the 2nd Virginia Cavalry, would remark, "Every time I went for the men, I played some prank on their whiskey, as I knew whiskey was to be blockaded soon and we would need it for the boys when they were sick." Such accounts are abundant, and demonstrate a prevailing Confederate awareness of the fact that siphoning off army whiskey meant denying it to their ailing comrades—a troubling prospect, but not necessarily prohibitive to drinking, as a veteran of the 12th Virginia Infantry Regiment by the name of George S. Bernard would sardonically recall:

> *The next morning, when, with the picket, I rejoined the regiment in bivouac, the late Maj. Daniel Lyon had already arrived there in a Jersey wagon, among the furnishings of which was an extremely plethoric demi-john of whiskey, chemically pure and of venerable age, which was intended for the sole consumption of the sick and wounded. I have no idea that John Lyon, or Tom Pollard, have yet forgotten how very sick we all were until relieved by a dose of that medicine.*

In short, medicinal whiskey did exist in Confederate camps, but its procurement was often accompanied by at least some measure of guilt, especially once the realities of blockade life set in. For the Union soldier, a swig of whiskey from the back of the surgical tent was seldom more than a harmless lark. To the Confederate, that same swig might expose a brother-in-arms to the hell of malaria, the horrors of amputation, or even the indignities of "Tennessee Quickstep," aka explosive diarrhea, without any form of chemical relief—a sobering thought, to say the least.

So where did the thirsty Confederate, longing for some small succor during the misery of war, find his guilt-free whiskey? Several means of procurement were at his disposal, none ideal, but all better than nothing . . . in most cases. With the South's alcohol supply running scarcer by the day, the demand for contraband whiskey soared. And high demand, as the eternal laws of economics dictate, is often accompanied by plummeting quality and soaring prices— both of which came to be the twin products of the North's bourbon blockade.

The most obvious method of getting whiskey, and generally the most common, was to resort to the local black market—an institution that thrived during wartime thanks to those blockade-runners and smugglers shrewd enough to exploit the liquor drought that plagued old Dixie. Southern whiskey at that point was indeed rare, but it still existed, and could be had for a price. And that price, during the darkest years of the war, was vertiginously steep. A gallon of good-quality whiskey in the winter of 1860 would have run the secession-minded Southerner a mere twenty-five cents. By 1863, that same gallon of spirits would break his bank at a whopping thirty-five *dollars*. And it wasn't just aged rye and smuggled bourbon that yielded to the immutable laws of supply and demand—even the rough stuff shot through the roof. Just look at what our Virginian friend Peck had to pay for a canteen of bootleg corn liquor:

> *There was a moonshiner a couple of miles from*
> *camp and a man was going there to get whiskey,*
> *so I gave him $5.00 to get a canteen filled for the*
> *quartermasters, fearing theirs would run out before*
> *the blockade was raised, and the man came back*
> *saying he couldn't get it for less than $10.00 a*
> *canteen.*

Elsewhere a soldier of the 2nd Tennessee Volunteers was reprimanded for drinking whiskey from his gun barrel after filling it illicitly at a nearby grocery, and Farwell Gould, one of the South's great heroes, once rode into battle with his whiskey jug in his arms, claiming that in the maelstrom of combat, "there wasn't no safe place to set it down." With whiskey, as with the war, what the Southerner lacked in resources and supplies, he did his best to make up for in determination and grit. And when he did manage to grab on to something, be it decent sipping whiskey or a strategic battlefield position, it proved exceedingly difficult to pry either from his hands.

With the price of smuggled and bootleg whiskey both wildly inflated, the resourceful Rebel could, in times of desperation, do the one thing that Union troops were seldom pressed to do: make his own. Many of those serving in the army of the Confederacy, and particularly those from Scots-Irish hill country, were already well acquainted with the whiskey still. With a makeshift still, such an individual could turn out a potent product that, while of suspect quality, did result in extreme intoxication, a fact attested to by the many colorful names such potations acquired—"Popskull," "Oh-be-joyful," "Old Red Eye," and "Nockum Stiff," to name a few. Recipes for these homemade concoctions could include anything from turpentine to rotten meat, unsavory additives intended to mimic the dark color and complex taste of genuine barrel-aged bourbon (a feat that was seldom accomplished, judging solely by those names, with very much success). The actual process of distilling, however, demanded free time, ample grain, and proper equipment, none of which was readily available to the hard-pressed armies of the Confederacy. The sheer difficulty of staying in one place for very long, with Grant and Sherman marching toward Richmond and Atlanta, limited the amount of whiskey even the most enterprising soldier could make.

And the last way for Lee's boys to get their hands on some whiskey? Well, just like Billy Yank, Johnny Reb did from time to time happen upon a whiskey still during the course of his marches, although opportunities to "commandeer" such whiskey were more limited. Knowing that stealing whiskey on his own soil would only serve to rob a fellow Southerner of his livelihood, Confederates were generally reluctant to pillage whiskey barrels while still in Dixie. However, on the rare occasions when the Southerner found himself in Yankee territory, he, like his Union counterpart, felt no compunction about "liberating" whiskey stores from the hands of the enemy. Kentucky, West Virginia, Maryland, and Pennsylvania each played host to invading Southern armies, and all had reputations for producing fine whiskey, with corn-based bourbon more prevalent in the first two states, and genuine rye the major product of the latter two. And as one can imagine, after getting by on medicinal swill, smuggled-in dregs, and homemade rotgut, your average Confederate was happy to have either. George S. Bernard, the Virginia infantryman we met earlier in the chapter, had the great fortune—and subsequent misfortune—of discovering a still while en route during General Lee's famous invasion of the North:

Our next adventure this morning was at a whiskey
still, at which dozens of Confederate soldiers
were filling themselves, their canteens, tin cups,
and everything else which would hold whiskey.
The scene at this still was very ludicrous, made
so by the eagerness of each man to get some of
the previous article and be off. Having filled our
canteens, we started with pleasant anticipation of
the joy our arrival would occasion among the boys
when they learned the contents of our canteens.
But unfortunately for our expectations, a guard
whom we encountered on the road a short distance
from the still very cooly took possession of each
man's canteen as he would come up and drain it of
whiskey.

Heartbreaking for George, but for us, an excellent
example of the great excitement Southern troops felt upon
discovering Northern whiskey, and the alacrity with which
said whiskey was recruited into their own canteens, almost
as if they were pilfering it directly from General Grant's
private stash. And when it came to raiding Union liquor
cabinets, the best chance the Rebs ever got may have been
on their field trip up north to a little town in Pennsylvania
called Gettysburg, with the whiskey charge being led by a
band of hard-drinking and harder-fighting men straight
from the Creole country of Louisiana. In an interesting bit
of historical irony, while the lads from Connecticut's Fighting Ninth were raising hell and dipping their cups in every
barrel on Bourbon Street, these bayou boys and wharf rats
were kindly returning the favor in the North, bringing the
fight to the Yankees and grabbing every drink of liquor
they could along the way. So let's close out this little com-
parative study of Civil War whiskey in style, with a grand

"Union & Rebel officers taking the last drink after signing the papers of parole &
exchange of prisoners," 1862. Some officers were more open-minded about
whiskey, and rewarded their weary troops after battle with a few healthy swigs.

finale supplied courtesy of one of the most colorful—
literally and figuratively—units from the entire war, a band
of bourbon-loving brigands from the Big Easy known by all
as the Louisiana Tigers.

The original 1st Special Battalion of the Louisiana
Volunteer Infantry was organized by Major Chatham
Roberdeau Wheat, gaining both battlefield distinction
and their famous sobriquet early in the war. The unit was
instantly recognizable thanks to their ferocious fighting
style and the pure brashness of their uniforms—the Tigers
donned the motley outfit of the fashionable French Zou-
aves, preferring fez caps and billowing red and blue para-
chute pants to the bland Confederate gray. Their ranks
were filled primarily by the rough-and-tumble manual
laborers of New Orleans and its environs, men who had
cut their teeth in the violent swamp-shack saloons of the
lower Mississippi and toughened their gullets on the
ample supply of bourbon and Monongahela whiskey that
could always be found there. And when it came to whiskey during wartime, Captain Jim Nisbet of the 21st Georgia Regiment would write that the "Louisiana Brigade, of
our Division, being mostly city or river men, 'knew the
ropes,' and could get it from Richmond." Evidently, the
Tigers were familiar with good whiskey, valued it highly,
and discovered how to procure it. It was a pronouncement
Captain Nisbet was in a good position to make—he was
once forced to break up a bloody brawl between his Geor-
gians and the Tigers over a bottle of stolen whiskey, and it
likely was only his intervention that prevented the tussle
from turning deadly.

This was all fine and well when smuggled bourbon was
within easy reach. But when the good stuff from the capital
wasn't available, the Tigers had no qualms about "living off
the land," and drinking up whatever Yankee whiskey hap-

pened to come their way. This strategy proved especially fruitful during the Gettysburg Campaign, when Confederate troops boldly invaded Northern soil. In the Pennsylvania town of York, they raided a clothing merchant and, upon discovering a store of aged whiskey, proceeded to "indulge in a great spree," with subsequent brawls occurring late into the night. While passing through Washington and Quincey townships, General Jubal Early anticipated trouble and sought to deprive the Tigers of looted alcohol by advising his officers to have "all intoxicating liquors put out of reach." Alas, he was not successful, and although local distillers and barkeeps buried whatever whiskey barrels the Confederate officers did not destroy, the Tigers dug them up, got liquored up, and not only began brawling, but also commenced stealing the clothes off the townspeople's backs, leaving them naked on the street. And it didn't stop there—the Tigers' hard boozing took them right into the heat of battle at Gettysburg, where a Private Ruch of Pennsylvania made the following observation of his Tiger opponents:

> *A little before sundown I saw a stir and a moving about of the Rebels under the window where I was sitting, as if they were getting ready for some kind of move. I also saw them drinking out of a barrel. The head of the barrel was knocked in. One would get a tin cup full and three or four would drink out of the same cup until it was empty. It could not have been water, for a tin of water would not have had so many drinks in it. It was straight whiskey, and they were getting ready to charge the Eleventh Corps.*

Whiskey in battle? When the Louisiana Tigers were involved, you'd better believe it. One color-bearer of the 8th

The famed Louisiana Tigers proved to be the South's fiercest—and thirstiest—fighters. This battlefield sketch depicts their whiskey-fueled assault on Cemetery Hill during the Battle of Gettysburg, 1863.

Louisiana Regiment was discovered by Union troops dead upon the field of battle with seven bullet holes in his body and a canteen clutched tightly between his fists. Inside the canteen was a peculiar mixture of gunpowder and whiskey, a cocktail that the Federal soldiers believed "accounted for his desperate bravery"—a fitting chaser and final drink for a true Louisiana Tiger.

But alas, despite the desperate bravery exhibited by the Southern forces at Gettysburg under the command of General Robert E. Lee, victory was not to be had. In their defeat during that audacious and failed invasion, the fate of the Confederacy became as sealed as its ports. As with whiskey, so went the war.

ON APRIL 9, 1865, at Appomattox Court House, Robert E. Lee—a gentleman fond enough of whiskey to know to avoid it—surrendered his saber, and the Confederacy, to Ulysses S. Grant, a warrior whose fondness for bourbon had caught the ear of the president himself. And if legend is to be believed, Frank and Jesse James, members of the notorious Quantrill guerrillas, tendered their own Confederate resignation on the front porch of T. W. Samuels, a Kentucky sheriff and whiskey distiller whose surname ought to be familiar to any enthusiast of Maker's Mark bourbon.* The war ended with far less bluster and bravado than that which had heralded its onset, as a battered and war-weary nation sought to come to terms with its ruined infrastructure and its mountains of dead. Many an American, regardless of allegiance, must have wondered as to the nature of the forces that had birthed such a cataclysm. They must have asked themselves how, in its furious wake, the tides of war had favored some and forsaken so very many more. These are questions as relevant and crucial today to our nation's history as they were when the shadow of the Civil War still lingered.

Easy answers will never come, but through the lens of the bourbon bottle, a clearer picture of the war's outcome

---

* Frank's .36 caliber Colt 1851 Navy cap-and-ball revolver is still on display at the Maker's Mark distillery. The Samuels family, who would later create Maker's Mark, were well acquainted with the James boys, and Bill Samuels Jr. often played with the revolver as a boy, a Kentucky variation on the all-American squirt gun.

emerges. In the North, we find an army with strategic control of crucial whiskey-producing border states, a firm grip on trading channels (i.e., rivers and coastal ports), and command of an industrial complex capable of augmenting the alcohol supply—not to mention weapons and war materials—as needed. In the South, on the other hand, we see a government crippled by blockade, limited in both manpower and resources, struggling to turn out moonshine while the bourbon still flowed utterly unimpeded in Northern cities like New York and Washington, D.C. And in an ironic twist of fate, the very cause of states' rights would prove to be a hindrance. When those in the central Confederate government realized their alcoholic disadvantage, they ordered Southern states to turn over whiskey stores and increase distillation; most of the states resisted, and some even enacted general prohibitions against distilling for the Confederate cause, preferring to keep their grain supply and whiskey barrels within their own borders. In many ways, the prevalence of the North and the valiantly contested but nevertheless inevitable surrender of the South was forecast in 1861, four years before Appomattox, when Kentucky's much-desired bourbon country, with its nation-nourishing rivers and railroads, was wrested from Polk's Confederates and left under Union control. And victory, although a long and bloody way off, came with it.

The American Civil War, with its four ruinous years and more than half a million lost lives, took a toll beyond reckoning on our nation. Yet the American Spirit that crawled coughing and cursing from the wreckage proved stronger, more unified, and more permanent than it had ever been before. From what had been a mob of quarrelsome states emerged one common national identity; and from a hodgepodge of amorphous distilleries rose a new class of bourbon makers more skilled, devoted, and conscious of their craft. In 1860, one estimate put the number of Kentucky distilleries at 207. By 1880, that total had dropped to 153, a drastic decline in the quantity of bourbon makers statewide. The distilleries that survived the privations of the war, however, proved to be those with the skill and savvy to adapt to a newer and more united United States of America. The fiery trials of wartime had a winnowing effect on the whiskey makers of the region; poorly managed distilleries were unable to stay open as before, and either folded completely or, as a result of Lincoln's steep excise tax on alcohol to fund the war effort, ditched their legitimacy and resorted to moonshining. What had formerly been an industry of small-timers seeking to make a little profit from leftover grain became, as a result of that winnowing process, a legitimate and serious business enterprise, led by the likes of D. M. Beam & Company, H. Wathen, Early Times, and J. W. Dant—names easily recognizable to the bourbon connoisseur today. And driven by postbellum opportunities, a scrappy new crop of entrepreneurial-minded candidates stepped to the distilling plate and took their swings, including an ambitious teenage boy left parentless and penniless by the war, just south of the Kentucky state line in Tennessee; his full name was Jasper Newton Daniel, but most of the folks around the way just called him Jack.

And so goes it: Just as a bone mends stronger after a break, the American Spirit proved resilient, and survived the war not only intact, but more firmly established than ever before. A thriving postwar economy brought new technologies and markets to a promising and uniquely American spirits industry. An entire segment of our country's population, previously relegated to the shameful status of property, could for the first time claim their rightful status as human beings and citizens, and enjoy liberties previously denied them, the legal purchase of bourbon whiskey among them.

And as we head toward the next chapter in our collective history, bourbon—just like America—is going to discover that prosperity comes with its own distinct set of challenges, no less destructive than a musket's ball. The age that awaits the American Spirit is a gilded one, full of tantalizing promise but equally replete with grimacing danger; beneath the wealth and riches lurk troubles that will test its integrity in whole new ways. . . .

5

Whiskey from a Gilded Glass

To HAVE DESCRIBED the Lindell Hotel in St. Louis as "opulent" would've been an understatement. "Palatial," equally inadequate. Simply calling it "gaudy" may have hit closer to the mark. By the 1870s, the town was booming, having transformed in only a few short decades from a muddy outpost to an industrial metropolis, well on its way to becoming the nation's fourth-largest city. And while St. Louis could claim to host a number of luxury hotels pandering to the waistcoated tycoons and industrial titans who stayed and played within their lavish walls, the Lindell took pride in besting them all. Built of Warrensburg gray sandstone in the Italianate style, it boasted with no small stridency Corinthian columns, richly carved trusses, and a two-story portico corniced in filigreed iron. Once within its imposing forty-five-foot-wide entrance, its illustrious guests were greeted by a chandeliered ballroom garnished with frescoes and tessellated marble—a place where, according to one contemporary observer, "everything that forethought could devise for the comfort of the guest and the facilitating of business had been provided." Far more than simply a place to spend the night, the Lindell functioned as the local "old boys club" for the industrial and political giants of the era. It was the place where coruscating fortunes could be made through winks and nods in backroom deals, with flambeau lamps and decanters of fine bourbon providing much of the illicit glow.

It goes without saying, then, that the Lindell Hotel had seen its share of celebrities, poseurs, and powerful men—it brought them about like flies to fresh meat. Yet even its normal show of exorbitance was rendered inconsequentially tame by the scenes that occurred there in the final days of February 1876. For it was precisely then, just down the street, that one of the more scandalous trials of the age concluded. Orville Elias Babcock—the private secretary to President Grant—escaped prosecution on corruption charges by the skin of his teeth, a feat made possible thanks only to Grant's personal and rather dubious testimony on his old war buddy's behalf.[*] When the eagerly awaited verdict came in, the entire courtroom erupted into a frenzy. As journalists from across the country sent frantic telegrams to break the big news, Mr. Babcock, along with a raucous mob of political heavy hitters and local industrialists—not to mention more than a few members of the allegedly "impartial" jury that had saved him—all paraded out from the judge's chambers and descended upon their familiar stomping grounds at the Lindell Hotel. Once assembled in its sparkling halls, they commenced the celebration by striking up a blaring brass

---

[*]   Many of the lower-level conspirators in the Whiskey Ring did not fare as well as Babcock—more than one hundred men were arrested during the course of the investigation, with more than $3 million in owed taxes recovered. One of the men apprehended was an inspector of internal revenue by the name of John McDonald, whose serialized version of events would help launch a young St. Louis publisher to fame and fortune. That young publisher's name? Joseph Pulitzer.

The sudden industrial prosperity that followed the Civil War ushered in a Gilded Age, for America and for bourbon whiskey. This 1870 engraving shows the "dining saloon of the hotel express train."

band and making a series of self-congratulatory toasts, many of which involved the very substance that had gotten them there: bourbon whiskey.

Well, *they* might have considered what they were selling to be bourbon whiskey. Those robustly jowled gentlemen with the ivory-handled canes and bespoke three-piece suits would have wanted it to pass as such, although many a true whiskey drinker would beg to differ. Not simply because of the massive amount of adulteration, dilution, and rectification that sullied their product, but because in many cases the product did not exist at all. Their little enterprise, which came to be known as the "Whiskey Ring," was a straight-up scam, a means by which dishonest distillers in cities like St. Louis, New Orleans, Chicago, and Cincinnati could not only turn out a cheap imitation of true barrel-aged Kentucky bourbon, but also make and sell a lot more of it than the government was aware. And even when the revenue agents did catch wind, the jig wasn't up—in fact, their scheme only became that much more criminal. The agents, along with many of the Republican officials they served, took massive bribes to keep the whole affair secret, depositing the tainted whiskey funds into their private bank accounts and party coffers. When Grant first learned of the Whiskey Ring's existence, he demanded an investigation. When that investigation led all the way back to his own private secretary, he ordered it squelched, although by then it was too late. The debacle that followed—complete with hired spies, deadly gangsters, warehouse brawls, and even secret telegrams from a shadowy figure code-named Sylph— would tarnish the reputation of the president and that of the United States government as a whole, at a time when both were increasingly assumed to be in the pocket of big business. And before any Democrats start shaking their fingers and patting themselves on the back, it deserves mention that their party was equally complicit and just as crooked. In fact, a whole new faction emerged in the wake of the Civil War, the Bourbon Democrats—the name a playful double entendre alluding to the whiskey, which by that time had become synonymous with exactly the sort of fat-cat corruption just mentioned, and also the amoral ostentation of the French Bourbon Dynasty. Needless to say, these were not

PROBE AWAY

In the wake of scandal and corruption, Uncle Sam
gives the bourbon industry a much-needed checkup.

bourbon's proudest days or finest hours. Nor our nation's,
for that matter.

But how did this happen? How did our hardscrabble
American Spirit, born of corn and honest sweat, come to be
by the late nineteenth century not merely an instrument of
corruption, but a veritable synonym for it? And with a reputation so dismally sullied, how on earth could it possibly be
redeemed? To answer these questions, we must take a closer
look at the growing pains racking our nation during its awk-

ward adolescence. A bourbon lover by the name of Mark Twain called it a "Gilded Age," and the whiskey he savored did not escape its false coat of corruption. The same innovations that fueled the coal, oil, and iron industries put steam in its stills; the same ill-gotten wealth that made giants of men beckoned its makers with equal seduction. Bourbon whiskey and the reputation time had given it both stood on the teetering brink—for our spirit to prevail and regain its true character, it would take the honest among its tenders to lend some character of their very own.

TO UNDERSTAND THE transformation sweeping the economic and social landscape of America in the decades following the Civil War—changes that would help a relatively inconsequential agrarian backwater become a spark-spurting, smoke-belching colossus—it is crucial to understand the character of the nation before men like Rockefeller, Carnegie, and Vanderbilt turned it into their own private Monopoly board. While these changes did happen quickly, they didn't happen overnight. Nor were they the result of any single invention or discovery. Rather, the metamorphosis was the culmination of a number of slow-brewing factors; a half-century's worth of technological innovations would have to meet the perfect mulch of mass urban markets and cheap urban labor for profits to grow and corruption to sprout. And in the 1870s and 1880s, the American climate was ripe for both to take root and positively flourish in ways that would alter our industrial complex at large, and the bourbon industry as well, albeit on a smaller scale.

At the close of the eighteenth century, when bourbon was first being produced as a commercial product in Kentucky, the manner of its making would have been easily

recognizable by the likes of George Thorpe, and probably even familiar to the Catalan Ramon Llull. The basic
techniques and equipment would have differed only
slightly from those that early European distillers used to
make spirits. The process did require skill, and certainly
experience, but it was at its essence a simple combination
of evaporation and condensation. There are tales of some
backwoodsmen using hollowed-out logs and even teaket-
tles and rags to distill strong corn spirit; however, the
most common method until the middle decades of the
nineteenth century was the traditional copper-pot still.
By running through that still a specially fermented distiller's beer made from cornmeal, jug yeast, and some
form of barley malt to turn the starch into sugar, the
Kentucky pioneer could very easily produce his own
whiskey, all thanks to one simple principle: alcohol boils
and evaporates at a lower temperature than water. By
carefully regulating the heat from his wood fire, he could
get the alcohol vapor to boil off the beer while minimizing the amount of water that evaporated with it. The
alcohol vapor then traveled up the neck of the still and
passed into the "worm," a coiled piece of water-cooled
copper tubing, where it quickly condensed back into a
liquid. The resulting spirit, at this point far more ethanol
than H_2O, could be collected in a steady drip. This first
distillate to come from the still was the "low wine." When
passed through the still again and distilled even further,
it acquired the name "high wine," and although raw and
un-aged, at this point the clear liquid could be called
whiskey. Not exactly rocket science, but science nonethe-
less. And while your average trans-Appalachian pioneer
of that era was lucky if he could sign his name, he under-
stood with uncanny intuition—as his Scots-Irish forefa-
thers did, and as many moonshiners do to this day—how

> *I* WANT TO PURCHASE
> Fifty barrels of GOOD WHISKEY,
> and pay for them in Boots & Shoes, with
> some cash.
>
> ### H. CRAWFORD.
> Boot & Shoe maker Main-Stree, Lex-
> ington.

Barter me this: In the early days of bourbon,
boots and shoes could be traded for barrels.

to coax the spirit out of the grain, thanks to a method
that had changed little in almost five hundred years.

The traditional, small batch distilling techniques of the
small Kentucky farmer were ones suited to the rhythms and
materials of the agrarian lifestyle that still dominated pre-
industrial America at the close of the eighteenth century.
For such farmers, it was a seasonal activity, a way of dis-
pensing with excess corn at the close of fall harvest. The
whiskey that resulted could be consumed by the farmer
himself, traded locally for everyday necessities like salt and
flour, or even bartered for somewhat loftier provisions, be
they earthly or celestial. In 1792, the stud fee for "the celebrated swift horse, Ferguson's Gray," was advertised as
nine shillings payable in merchantable whiskey, and in
1798, a minister by the name of John Shackelford was
promised, "as compensation for his services," thirty-six
gallons of Kentucky corn spirit—some indication of the
fine line that whiskey trod then, as it so often does today,
between perdition and the pulpit. Regardless of how it was
spent, however, the bourbon of that era was far more of an
agricultural by-product than an intentioned commodity; it

was a means by which the small farmer might find some assistance in acquiring his staples, or at the very least, in finding some amusement with friends during the cold months of winter. And although a few early distillers such as Elijah Pepper, Evan Williams, and Jacob Beam did begin their incipient commercial efforts in the late eighteenth century, most of the whiskey produced at that time would not have been for "commercial" purposes in the modern sense that we know them. Few among us would dare drop an airline bottle of Beam in the Sunday offering basket, nor would the investor from Dubai be likely to acquire his derby stallion with handles of Jack Daniel's. Bourbon in those days was a cottage industry at best, and intoxication aside, it served a very different purpose from the whiskey we know today—or at least it did prior to the arrival of the nineteenth century.

As to whether demand spurred new technology or new technology encouraged demand, there will always be a sort of chicken-and-egg debate. But what is certain is that by the first few decades of the 1800s, the early innovations of a nascent Industrial Revolution made their way to bourbon country, and coincidently right alongside with them, a rising class of true commercial distilleries. In 1794, Alexander Anderson of Philadelphia patented a steam still, followed in 1801 by a patent for a perpetual still—two inventions that altered for the first time in half a millennium the basic nature of spirit distillation. Newfangled steam power, fueled by coal rather than cordwood, could be used to quickly and accurately heat the mash to the desired temperature; even more important, thanks to the perpetual still, which could be fed a steady stream of "wash"—also known as distiller's beer—a continuous stream of alcohol could be produced as well. By 1815, these patented steam-powered perpetual stills were being used as far west as

Kentucky, and by 1818 they had nearly taken over. That very year, our familiar distilling chronicler Harrison Hall would write, "The old way of distilling is generally pursued only by such as work upon a small scale, or are unwilling to be at the expense of a patent right." Proof that by the end of the century's first two decades, the old-fashioned pot still was already going the way of the dodo bird, at least as far as commercial distilleries were concerned. And as if that weren't enough, in 1830, Aeneas Coffey introduced the world to his "column" still, an advanced variant of Anderson's perpetual still capable of distilling three thousand gallons of wash in a single hour. And you don't need a mathematician to tell you that such a quantity adds up to a whole lot of bourbon.[*]

While the material advancements increased the sheer volume of bourbon a distillery could turn out, it would take equally radical improvements in technique to regulate that output and make it consistent. And for that, the newborn bourbon industry would owe a Scotsman by the name of Dr. James C. Crow a tremendous debt of gratitude. The folksy name belies a serious scientific mind—no mere country doctor, Crow studied medicine and chemistry at Edinburgh University before immigrating to Kentucky in 1823, where he applied his genius directly to whiskey. First at the Glenn's Creek distillery, and later at Old Oscar Pepper, he took what had been a haphazard procedure and applied to it a scientific method. Whereas the old distillers had dipped

---

[*] Interesting side note: It wasn't just booze that was getting bigger when it came to the vice department. Thanks to the new technologies of the Industrial Revolution, James Bonsack was able to patent a machine that could make 120,000 cigarettes in ten hours. This was at a time when the very best cigarette rollers could only turn out about 3,000 in a day. Sad days for professional cigarette rollers, but a boon for future generations of chain smokers.

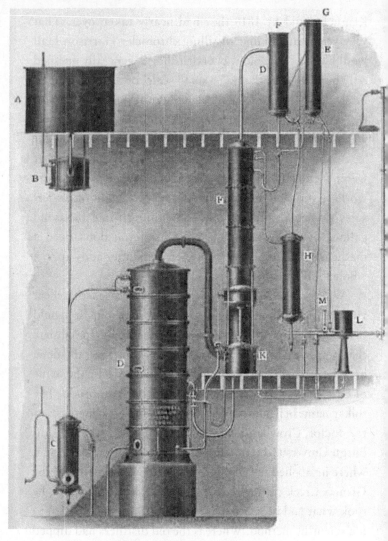

Coffey's new column still was a far cry from the
humble pot stills that gave birth to bourbon.

For much of the nineteenth century,
Old Crow was *the* name in bourbon whiskey.

in a finger and given it a lick, he used saccharimeters to gauge the sugar content of the mash and thermometers to regulate its temperature, and took careful measurements of acidity levels throughout. His greatest contribution was without a doubt the introduction of the sour mash process for regulating batch consistency; by adding a small quantity of leftover mash (the mixture of grain, malt, water, and yeast that makes distiller's beer) from the previous batch, he was able to regulate pH levels in each run of the still, enabling consistency of product on a larger scale. His methods were enthusiastically adopted by other big distilleries, and by his death in 1856, it had become commonplace in bourbon distillation, as it still is to this day. His legacy would live on not just in practice, but also in name—remember the Old Crow bourbon that the likes of Grant and Twain were so fond of? It was named after him. So great was Crow's influence that the *New York Times*, nearly a half-century after his death, would write that "to him, more than to any other man, is due the international reputation that Kentucky whiskey enjoys, and the vast distilling interests of the country are largely the result of his discoveries." The invention of bigger and more efficient stills may first have enabled whiskey production on a massive scale, but the whiskey they produced was palatable and salable thanks to the scientific techniques that Dr. James C. Crow pioneered.

With the introduction of advanced steam-powered stills and the implementation of improved quality-control methods in the first decades of the nineteenth century, the bourbon industry was poised for expansion and ready for the big time. With only one small problem: The rest of America had yet to catch up. Because despite what you may have heard about Kentucky down at the stereotype mill, the big bourbon-producing distilleries in the north and central portion of the state were actually ahead of their time when it came to industrial innovation—so much, in fact, it proved in some cases to their detriment. A good example of this is the massive Hope Distillery in Louisville, Kentucky. The complex boasted advanced machinery, power-driven stirring rakes, and a gargantuan imported still with a capacity of 1,500 gallons, powered by a high-tech 45-horsepower steam engine. By 1821, it was churning out well over 1,000 gallons a day in whiskey, with only one small problem—they had run out of people willing to pay to drink it. Hampered by problems of demand and distribution, the distilling complex had simply outgrown its time and place; it was producing more whiskey than anyone locally needed. Whiskey distilleries were getting bigger, but at a rate that far outpaced their market and distribution infrastructure. But how could there possibly be too much whiskey? Take a critical look at these two similar real estate listings from editions of the *Western Citizen* appearing in the

1850s, and see if the answer doesn't jump off the page . . . or at least paddle slowly across it:

> A Large Brick Steam Distillery, capable of making 3
> Barrels of Whisky per day, the whole year. There is an
> abundance of Cold Spring Water to run the Distillery the
> driest time ever known in Kentucky; and a ready market,
> at a fair price, for all the Whisky that can possibly be
> made. And there is perhaps no place in Kentucky where
> CORN can be produced as cheap, and as conveniently
> for a Distillery, as at this point, the River affording ample
> facilities for the transportation of both Corn and Whisky.
> Steamboats pass the property from six to eight months in
> the year.

And yet another listing in another Kentucky county that includes:

> [A]n excellent wharf perfectly convenient for the
> landing of coal, wood, grain, etc., and equally so for
> the shipping of everything either up or down the river.
> The improvements consist of a large three story stone
> warehouse, a still-house, woodhouse, and excellent pens.
> The machinery is of the best and most approved patterns
> for making copper distilled Whisky, the engine is a
> splendid one and entirely new, having cost a few months
> since, one thousand dollars. The establishment is supplied
> by a splendid spring of pure water which never fails and
> never gets muddy.

The two distillery grounds listed for sale have much in common—steam power, modern buildings, advanced machinery, and the latest in high-volume stills. Indeed, one can practically smell the new copper, all gleaming, fresh and ready. But there is something else they share that renders the first advert's claim of a "ready market" for "all the Whisky that can possibly be made" somewhat suspect. And what might that be? Water. No, not the lime-rich springwater, although that is crucial for good bourbon, but rather the rivers they use for transporting the finished product. It's the 1850s, boilers are hissing, steam engines are humming, scientific instruments are dutifully gauging their progress, yet the means of getting those bourbon barrels to thirsty customers haven't changed since the days of Daniel Boone. Granted, steam power did mean that paddleboats could go upriver as well as down, which opened up markets in ports like St. Louis and Minneapolis, but effectively, bourbon bound for distant saloons and groceries had to follow the same tortuous route instated in the 1700s: a bobbing journey along the Ohio River, a long, muddy slog down the Mississippi, a piling onto ships in New Orleans, a nauseating voyage on the high seas, and an eventual landing in port cities like New York, Philadelphia, Charleston, and Savannah. This excruciatingly long haul was what made bourbon oak-aged in the first place. And it was still the primary means of transporting bourbon prior to the Civil War.

Following the Civil War, however, the introduction of a national rail system changed everything. The culmination of advancements in steam engines, steel production, coal mining, and telegraph technology, the railroads altered the face of America, and forever transformed our cultural concept of distance. And although functioning steam-engine locomotives had existed since the early nineteenth century right alongside the first steam-powered stills, our national rail system would not truly blossom until the realization of the economic and industrial growth spurt that occurred immediately after the Civil War. In 1865, the network of iron and steel rails in America extended a meager 35,000 miles; by 1870, in just five

Riding the rails: The emergence of the railroads in the
late nineteenth century greatly expanded bourbon's market.

years, it had grown to 53,000 miles. In 1880, some 93,000
miles of track were at the beck and call of America's industrialists, and by 1890, that number reached 164,000 miles. The
trains that ran along these tracks were carrying ten billion
tons of freight per mile of track in 1865, and seventy-nine billion tons per mile by 1890. And coupled with this dizzying
expansion was a dramatic drop in cost—in the last year of the
Civil War, a ton of freight cost an average of two cents a mile
to ship. By the end of the century, the cost would fall to three-
quarters of a cent, making shipping by rail the fastest, cheap-
est, and smartest way to transport anything heavy—including
five-hundred-pound bourbon barrels—more than a few miles.
Industry in America took on incredible new dimensions, and
the heavily wooded backwater of frontier settlements and

quaint little port cities it had been only a few years before would be forever changed because of it.

As for bourbon, with transportation and markets finally catching up to its stills, our American Spirit had nowhere to go but up.* While the industrial production of crude petroleum jumped from 0.5 million tons in 1860 to 45.8 million tons in 1900, and crude steel from .01 million tons to 11.2 million, corn production grew right along with it, leaping from 838.8 million bushels in 1860 to 2.7 billion bushels in 1900. And more corn meant more whiskey. The value of total distilled spirits in 1860 was $26 million; twenty years later, $41 million. And by the end of the century? Ninety-six million dollars, a fortune by modern standards, a cash cow with unlimited udders in the dollars of those days. Everything for bourbon was at last coming together, and it all was inextricably linked, including the connection between industry and new markets. Because those urban plants and factories needed workers to run them, and those want ads attracted migrants and immigrants galore. In 1850, only 15 percent of Americans lived in urban territory; by the century's end, almost half of Americans lived in cities, many of those new urbanites having arrived via a second great surge of foreign immigration that coincided nicely with the country's fresh need for cheap industrial labor. And our population as a whole? It exploded. In that same half-century time span, the number of people living in the United States more than tripled, from twenty-three million to seventy-six million. And in that number were an awful lot of thirsty

---

* Speaking of bourbon going up, another technological advancement of the era was the invention of the modern drinking straw in 1888 by Marvin C. Stone—he had grown tired of sucking up his mint juleps through hollow stalks of ryegrass, as was the custom at that time. Sadly, Mr. Stone would pass away in 1899, and would not live to see the invention of the bendy straw or the crazy straw, both of which came about in the twentieth century.

Irishmen, Italians, Germans, Slavs, and Jews all eager to become Americans, and more than eager to end a hard day at the mill by bellying up to the bar and tossing back a truly American drink. Bourbon—and America—were growing up.

While science did standardize and codify the making of fine bourbon whiskey, the technique of it was still then, as it is today, far more craft than chemistry lesson. First, there's the essential Kentucky springwater, sweet on the tongue and rich in lime. That must be mixed with just the right proportion of ground corn, barley malt, and in some cases rye or wheat, to produce a wash worthy of becoming whiskey. This mixture must be gently cooked and methodically stirred, traditionally in a tub of American cypress wood, before the grain may invite the yeast. When the consistency is just right, and the temperature neither too hot nor too cold, a special strain of jug yeast is finally added, and given time to gently bubble its way through the corn-sweetened mixture, creating a heady aroma akin to ale and freshly baked bread. And once that original corn porridge has successfully become beer, it is fed into a still and heated in a way that provokes the intoxicating essence to travel upward and reconvene in chilled copper. This process is repeated until the resultant pure, clear wine is at an adequate proof, at which point it is stored inside white oak barrels with interiors charred by flame. Casked as such, the spirit is given time to rest in darkened warehouses, and over a period of years, the oaken staves, expanding and contracting through the warm Kentucky summers and cold Kentucky winters, will relieve the whiskey of impurities, and add rich tannins all its own. On several occasions during the maturation process, a master distiller will probe the barrel's contents with a device known as a "whiskey thief," withdrawing a few drops to taste. And once the contents are deemed fit, he will bestow upon the whiskey the title of bourbon.

Trade publications from the Gilded Age give some indication
of just how big a business bourbon had become.

Such is the almost allegorical beauty of making fine whiskey, and crafting true bourbon—an art form passed down from master to apprentice, father to son, teacher to student, over the course of generations. It's the way the very finest bourbons have always been made. And just as an expert winemaker can identify a specific vintage or valley by the aroma of the grape, so could the finest bourbon distillers identify a whiskey's home spring or hollow; those humble men who helped bourbon gain its well-founded reputation as fine whiskey knew neither molecular science nor macroeconomics, but when it came to producing exquisite bourbon, they were masters of their craft.

In the latter half of the nineteenth century, however, bourbon and its time-honored traditions began to change— at least at many distilleries. For while making fine bourbon took patience and skill, turning out cheap brown liquor required little more than food coloring and a still. With the introduction of mass production and mass markets into traditional whiskey making, there was suddenly money—big and easy money—to be made in the business. And whatever little government regulation existed could easily be circumvented, bought off, or brought right in and made a full partner in crime. So much potential profit and so little oversight had a naturally deleterious effect on the industry. The decades of the 1870s and 1880s would see the American whiskey trade beset by all manner of corruption and scams, and the toll they would take on bourbon's reputation would damage it almost—*almost*, but as is so often the case in America, not quite—beyond repair.

The foremost and most press-worthy of the whiskey scams of the Gilded Age were those that occurred on a broad, financial scale, generally involving collusion of some form between the government bodies that regulated whiskey distilling and the distillers themselves. The Whiskey Ring that began our chapter serves as the most glaring example of such white-collar whiskey crimes, and even John McDonald, the Treasury Department official who ended up taking the rap, admitted that "no ring was ever before formed embracing such a gigantic scope and including among its chief instigators and membership, such distinguished Government officials." And the man had a point—once the whole nasty business saw daylight during the U.S. Grand Jury testimony, a trail of damning evidence was slowly revealed that led all the way to the front steps of the White House itself. During the questioning that followed, President Grant was struck by an exceedingly dubious strain of amnesia, some indication of just how high up the corruption had reached. The Whiskey Ring was broken up in the end, with more than a few members of the top brass narrowly escaping prison, but that proved hardly the deterrent that prosecutors envisioned.

A mere decade later, a like-minded "Whiskey Trust" was formed by a number of powerful midwestern businessmen to artificially manipulate the prices of distilled spirits. Their nefarious schemes culminated in the 1891 arrest of the distilling magnate George J. Gibson for plotting to destroy a rival distillery, and the indictment two years later of the Trust's directors for illegally restraining trade. Once again, the charges proved of little consequence to the orchestrators; those with money and connections could operate more or less with impunity, and in classic Hydra fashion, for every big scam broken up, a cluster of smaller ones would appear in its place. Simply by keeping abreast of tax increases from "friends" in Washington, whiskey distillers could alter their output to maximize profits. And thanks to a legal loophole in which existing "aging" whiskey was exempt from mounting taxes, virtually anyone could purchase blocks of stored whiskey at as little as eighteen cents a gallon and make a killing in speculation. At one point, it was estimated that the whiskey industry was squirreling away at least forty million gallons—equal to a year's supply for the entire United States at that time—as a means of circumventing the system and getting filthy rich.* The stuff of Kentucky woodsmen and frontier cabins? Hardly. This was straight-up Gordon Gekko territory, and people were amassing fortunes at the expense of bourbon's good name.

The big-money scams may have consumed the most headline ink in the yellow journalism that ruled the day, but a far more pedestrian form of whiskey swindle proved far more prolific. For while *nouveau riche* distilling magnates and crooked politicians might toast each fresh windfall with the very finest barrel-aged bourbon, they had few qualms about selling a very different class of product to the unwashed masses. And adding insult to this bourbon-based injury, many of the middlemen and liquor distributors had even fewer qualms about degrading the whiskey even further. With only limited industrial regulation, and quality control totally at the distiller's discretion, it took no time at all for whiskey producers without scruples— and there were a ton—to figure out that they could sell a shoddy, second-class product at a minimal cost and claim it as true bourbon.

To do so, however, did require some skill. The "art," if one may even deign to call it that, of turning cheap mass-produced grain alcohol into something resembling good, drinkable whiskey, relied on the practices of "adulteration" and "compounding." Both were techniques for manipulating the low-grade spirit with additives and chemicals to hoodwink the drinker and render it more palatable. Both were

---

* In 1880, Congress excused the entire whiskey industry from taxes on spirit that had evaporated during barrel aging, an act that saved distillers a considerable amount of money. Legend attributes this nice little bonus, commonly known as the "Carlisle Allowance," to a card game between John G. Carlisle of Kentucky and the soon-to-be president Grover Cleveland. Guess who won?

commonplace among distillers in the Gilded Age of the late nineteenth century. An 1889 distilling manual written by Leonard Monzert treats the practices in depth, with a troubling nonchalance that hints at just how ubiquitous they truly were. Far from being fringe treatments utilized by the most scurrilous of distillers, Monzert writes, "this branch of the business is very extensive and has reached such perfection that experts are also deceived." The form of liquor legerdemain most commonly exercised by these whiskey Svengalis was that of imitating or artificially re-creating the aging process crucial to fine bourbon. According to Monzert:

The art of artificially imparting qualities to new wines and liquors, identical with those produced by age, as well as the reproduction of chemical compounds, requires not only tact and skill but a certain amount of practical expertise, and a thorough knowledge of the composition of alcoholic products.

Tact and skill? Wait, it gets better:

Producers cannot afford to wait so long a time, and there being no demand from consumers for the newly distilled liquors, they are obliged to dispose of their product to what we in this country call Compounders, *or* Rectifiers, *and in France* Fabricants, *or (vulgarly)* empoisonneurs, *which means poisoners.*

Telling, indeed, is his use of the term "poisoner," as these tricksters had all sorts of foul means at their disposal for doctoring garbage-grade whiskey and disguising it as good bourbon. Looking to add an artificial bead to your ersatz booze?

Try "sweet oil and sulphuric acid." Want your whiskey a little more astringent? "Cream of tartar, acetic acid, acetic ether" can all do the trick. If the spirit's too sallow, a little "burnt sugar" and "black tea boiled thirty minutes" should suffice, and if it's that good old "bed-bug flavor" you're after—whatever the hell that is—good Sir Monzert suggests adding "a few drops of strong ammonia in a barrel of liquor." Needless to say, these were not the sort of scientific advancements Dr. James C. Crow had in mind when he packed up his chemistry set and moved to Kentucky. These were cheap tricks for creating a knockoff product and selling it at a premium price.

While the shameful practices of compounding and adulterating were visited upon the spirit by the distillers, even greater ignominies awaited it once packaged and sent out the door. Whiskey in those days was shipped to distributors and vendors as it had been for almost a century: in barrels. And porous wood sealed only by a cork bung was hardly tamper-proof packaging. Upon exiting the distiller, gauger, or rectifier, each barrel was essentially fair game for anyone who handled it. The whiskey contained within, whether it was fine Kentucky bourbon or something similar from beyond the Bluegrass, was at the mercy of any unscrupulous wholesaler, grocer, or tavern owner who acquired it. The contents could be watered down, re-blended, and in many cases replaced with a completely different inferior product. During an investigation of the whiskey market by the Committee on the Judiciary of the House of Representatives, Joseph B. Greenhut—the head of the notorious Whiskey Trust previously mentioned—confessed that his powerful whiskey monopoly had "no control" over its distributors, and that even low-grade whiskey could be sold "for anything they please," and labeled with "any fancy name they want." For the sake of efficiency, whiskey makers became highly reliant on these sorts of regional distributors—Old Jordan

Many of the whiskeys claiming to be true barrel-aged bourbon didn't pass the smell test—or laboratory inspection, for that matter.

bourbon was handled by W. H. Thomas & Son in Louisville, and Cedar Brook bourbon was the sole province of James Levy & Bro. in Cincinnati—and once the whiskey was under their control, what actually became of it was anyone's guess.

As if that wasn't injurious enough to bourbon's reputation, further damage was often inflicted by the saloon keepers and grocers who procured the barrels from the distributors; not only were they prone to diluting and mislabeling a barrel's contents, they were able to do so with little fear of the consequences. In the 1880s, a barkeep by the name of Pat Mallon of New York City was charged with selling watered-down whiskey to his patrons. Ultimately, however, the judge ruled in Mallon's favor—as the dishonest publican had paid full price to acquire the original whiskey, there was no law preventing him from selling it however he saw fit. Scams of this sort would be repeated and perpetrated time and time again, in liquor-based establishments across the country. Without oversight or regulation, and with a quick buck on the mind of nearly everyone who handled it, it's no wonder the American Spirit took it right on the chin. Ordering a glass of the good stuff became akin to a game of Russian roulette, with the liquid in question as likely to be ethanol mixed with food coloring and ammonia as it was true oak-aged bourbon. And increasingly, it was a game consumers were not especially inclined to play.

With the German-American beer companies of the Midwest able to provide a more "wholesome" and less taintprone product, and the temperance movement in America's heartland beginning to stir, our national spirit was under serious threat. Dark days for bourbon, and for America as well, as corruption, greed, and scandal threatened the integrity of both. Mark Twain was right—beneath the gold and the glitter loomed something ominous and grotesque, and by the late nineteenth century, the sheen that had cloaked it was beginning to peel away, revealing for all the dismal truth beneath. Something needed to be done, and in the hills and hollows of bourbon's birth country lived a handful of courageous men determined enough to do it.

UPON TRAVERSING THE countryside of Kentucky's Bourbon Trail on a crisp autumn day, with the sky bright and clear and the changing leaves a ripened auburn, an undeniable fact slowly emerges: The place that bourbon calls home is not so terribly large. Not in terms of raw distance, although the various distillery signs one passes among tobacco barns and horse fields are seldom more than a few miles apart. But more in the remarkable proximity one feels between the residents and their history—the sense that with bourbon, it is indeed a very small world. Many of the people you meet will come from families that trace their roots to the earliest days of the region's pioneer settlements. More than a few of them will have close personal ties to local bourbon distilleries that go back generations. And should you venture to the Old Talbott Tavern in Bardstown for a quiet glass of Blanton's followed by a tumbler of Knob Creek, as I recently did, there's even a decent chance you will encounter individuals who go on hunting trips and church picnics with the prominent distilling families of the town, and who know the master distillers on a first-name basis. Such individuals will welcome you in warm and generous tones, and will speak intimately of legendary figures ranging from Oscar Pepper all the way down to Booker Noe as if close family friends—which in many cases, they actually were. At the intersection of family, history, and craft, you will find bourbon, and among the locals for whom the word means more than just a drink, a deep and intensely personal pride in the traditions that surround it.

Such is the bond between Kentuckians and their heritage, and it was as prevalent and pervasive in the late nineteenth century as it is today. The sins of the politicians and industrial distillers did not go unnoticed or unchallenged by those who saw bourbon as far more than an easy way to make a buck. Not that the family distillers of the Bluegrass were not interested in profit—they most certainly were, as bourbon makers had been, in some form or another, since its inception. It was more that they recognized the need for a delicate compromise between modernization and legacy; they recognized the imperative nature of bourbon's integration into the industrial era, but were strongly of the conviction that the quality and care that had established it as the American Spirit need not be compromised in the process. When U.S. secretary of the treasury Benjamin Bristow was first getting whiffs of something fishy in the whiskey distilleries of river ports like St. Louis and Cincinnati, it was a delegation of "Western" whiskey makers "known by the department to be honest" that described the schemes of the nefarious Whiskey Ring and urged its destruction. When the notorious Whiskey Trust began crushing the competition and flooding the market with inferior product, the charge against it was again led by the bourbon makers of Kentucky. True, they did have a financial interest in disrupting the industrial distilleries that so readily undersold them, but it was more than that—the low-grade whiskey the big whiskey barons churned out, and the dishonest distribution practices that accompanied it, were direct affronts to the bourbon they cherished and the families that made it. And that, they would not stand for. Through tactful marketing and strategic innovation, a handful of honest bourbon distillers in the spirit's Kentucky homeland were able to make a difference.

The first and most obvious means of deterring the common practice of tampering with whiskey once it was out of the distiller's hands was to resolve the packaging problem—a conundrum first tackled, interestingly enough, by a young pharmaceutical salesman out of Louisville with a taste for fine bourbon named George Garvin Brown. Whiskey in that era, as it had been in the Civil War before—indeed, even back to the days of medieval Gaelic monks—was commonly viewed as having both curative and restorative powers. The medicinal marijuana of its day, it was prescribed by doctors, often with a wink and a nod, to those suffering from ailments with no other ready treatment or cure. Mr. Brown, with his practice in pharmaceuticals and local ties to the bourbon industry, was especially interested in selling medicinal whiskey to doctors in the area. The only problem? While an impoverished and exhausted immigrant laborer might suffer a phony, potentially even toxic shot of bourbon whiskey at the end of a hard day, medical professionals were not especially inclined to prescribe to their patients a course of treatment containing God knows what from God knows where. In order to reassure his medical market, George Garvin Brown needed a solution to the barreling issue—one that he found in the form of glass bottles. Easier to seal and more difficult to tamper with, the narrow-necked glass whiskey bottle we know today was first pioneered by Brown in 1870, when he began selling his Old Forester bourbon not by the oak barrel, but by the bottle, seeing such a step as one toward righting an industry that had gone morally astray. The process took a while to catch on, as bottling practices of this nature were not cheap, but as technology caught up with the demand, other bourbons— Old Crow among them—began following his lead, and offering consumers a product that at the very least was far less likely to have been adulterated, watered down, or

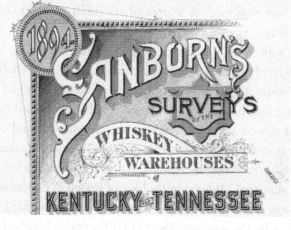

To combat inferior, counterfeit "bourbon" from the industrial Midwest, the distilleries of Kentucky and Tennessee had to organize and stick together. This 1894 survey lists approximately five hundred distilleries and whiskey warehouses in the region.

flat-out poisoned. A source of no small comfort, to say the least.*

With the immediate issue of barrel tampering being addressed, the next logical step was to find a way to challenge the power and authority of the whiskey barons who had been filling said barrels with such questionable ethics and liquor. And this meant directly taking on the powerful and aforementioned Whiskey Trust that had come to dominate the spirits industry in the late nineteenth century, ruthlessly led from the industrial Midwest by the likes of Joseph B. Greenhut and George J. Gibson. The effort was captained by another Louisvillian by the name of Thomas H. Sherley, a bourbon man and an investor with interests in the New Hope Distilling Company. Ruthless in his own right, Sherley had gained a reputation as a fierce proponent and defender of bourbon whiskey, even going so far as to take a small-time liquor dealer from Boston all the way to the Massachusetts Supreme Court for welshing on one hundred barrels of bourbon shipped from Kentucky. He would later take his tenacity and devotion to a whole new level when he helped unify fifty-nine local bourbon distilleries to form the Kentucky Distilleries and Warehouse Company, a direct response to the Whiskey Trust's consolidated power, and a recognition of the ancient truth that there was indeed strength in numbers. The members of his bourbon league followed the traditional pot still method of distilling, and eschewed the shady blending and adulterating practices that the large commercial distilleries of the Whiskey Trust embraced. Sherley, along with the Kentucky Distilleries Com-

---

* Speaking of comfort, Brown would later attempt to mollify the local ladies of the temperance movement by publishing at his own expense *The Holy Bible Repudiates "Prohibition,"* a collection of biblical passages that spoke favorably of alcohol, compiled for those as predisposed to tipping the wrist as to turning the other cheek.

pany he helped create, contested the monopolistic practices of the Whiskey Trust and lobbied for legislation to differentiate their true spirit from the subpar product that the Trust's distillers sold as bourbon.

A *New York Times* article from 1897 sums up rather nicely Sherley's objectives:

> *A movement is on foot among the Kentucky distillers of Bourbon whisky to organize a trust, in opposition to the American Spirits Company, makers of high wines, popularly known as the Whisky Trust. . . . The object of the proposed association is to make Bourbon whisky which is matured by age, instead of chemicals, a distinct commodity from cheaper liquor. The movement has been started by circulars sent out by Thomas H. Shirley [sic] of the New Hope Distilling Company, as the result of a meeting in this city a few days ago. The movement is practically to enlarge the scope of the Kentucky Distillers' Association, and if it succeeds will bring about a separation of the Bourbon whisky from high wines and spirits which are sold through the high wine trust as whisky. . . . There is little danger of a war between the two, as what is mostly desired is that the two classes of liquors should be distinguished.*

The ever-insightful writers of the *New York Times* were absolutely correct in deducing the motives of Thomas H. Sherley and his assembly of Kentucky bourbon distillers. They were somewhat less astute, however, when they stated that there was "little danger of a war between the two." The Whiskey War, as it came to be known, was already well under way by 1897, and while Sherley proved to be an admirable general, the commander in chief of the struggle to save bourbon was a man whose forward thinking and creative genius would not only rescue the spirit from its Gilded Age quagmire but usher it fully into the modern era.

Which brings us to the last, although certainly not least, of our triumvirate of Gilden Age bourbon champions, a cultivated Kentuckian by the name of Edmund Haynes Taylor. Long before Harland Sanders was donning string ties and peddling poultry, "Colonel" Taylor was taking a native Kentucky product and enlivening it with an ingenious flair for marketing and a savvy approach to brand identity. One of the first true bourbon aristocrats, he would run seven different distilleries over his career, including such famous tipples as Old Crow, Old Pepper, Old Taylor, and Old Fire Copper—all highly respected bourbons at that time. His greatest accomplishment was bringing to bourbon the concept of branding, imbuing each label with a character of its own. Whereas Dr. James C. Crow had made bourbon commercially viable through scientific innovation, Taylor furthered that legacy by making it marketable in a highly competitive whiskey field. No friend to the indifferent methods of the Whiskey Trust and their ilk, he would lament the arrival of "carelessly made whiskeys, whose aim is quantity and whose objective is mere chaffing for cheapness," and bemoan how "the quality recedes as the cheapness advances. . . . The ancient Bourbon flavor has departed." His method of combating them, true to his genius, was through branding. While a vague notion of advertising-specific bourbon brands had existed for half a century—a distiller by the name of Solomon Kellar was famous for pitching his distinctive Kellar brand whiskey as early as 1849—most bourbon makers invested little time or energy in differentiating their bourbon from the competitors'. All of which changed with E. H. Taylor. He invoked the unique qualities of fine Kentucky bourbon in the new forms of advertisements and pamphlets he produced, and he purposefully promoted his brands by name, with distinct marketing strategies for each. He even went so far as to establish his Old Taylor distillery as a legitimate tourist attraction and vehicle for public relations, complete with reception rooms, a Roman-columned springhouse, and a medieval castle. To what end? Well, to lend each of his brands a sense of quality and distinction that the inferior whiskeys produced by the industrial distilleries of the Midwest were lacking. And thanks to the political connections he accrued in the process, he would prove instrumental in the passage of two of the most important, preventative, and ultimately restorative acts of legislation of that era.

The combined efforts of bourbon whiskey's three most prominent champions of the era—Brown, Sherley, and Taylor—culminated in the Bottled-in-Bond Act of 1897, and the Pure Food and Drug Act that passed less than a decade later. The former established a government-certified seal of authenticity for packaged whiskey, and allowed bourbon to be readily bottled and marketed in store windows with stamped assurance that its contents were as the snappily designed labels claimed. The latter, perhaps even more significantly, at last defined what constituted real bourbon, and officially differentiated it from its cheaper blended competition. Thanks to the aggressive lobbying and ardent testimony of Kentucky's bourbon leadership, their cherished product at last had government protection guarding its integrity and guaranteeing its good name. Gone were the days of low-quality knockoffs claiming to be Kentucky's finest, and barrels with unknown chemicals sloshing within—Uncle Sam had at last stopped counting his money bags, and finally got back to the business of doling out justice. This was the

The Old Taylor Distillery of Frankfort, Kentucky,
was one of the first to bring branding to the bourbon game,
creating a distinct identity that set its label apart.

birth of the Progressive Era in America, one of political activism and social reform, born from a national desire to rub off the phony gold spray paint of the Gilded Age and get back to something honest and real. The American Spirit, having at last reconciled its industrial growth spurt with the moral integrity it had so nearly lost, was almost ready for the twentieth century.

Almost, mind you. Because before bourbon can settle its spurs fully in the modern world, there are still a few wild corners of the country left to be tamed, and still a fair number of whiskey drinkers out on the range who know more about six-shooters than they do about stock prices. And thanks to these newfangled railroads, getting there is only a hop, skip, and a few whistle-stops away. So saddle up and get ready, because the West didn't get Wild by sipping Coca-Cola, and America didn't cut its teeth on Dentyne gum. Long before there was a car in every driveway and a chicken in every pot, there was a saloon on every corner and a bullet with your name on it.

Hi-yo, bourbon! Away!

6

How the West Was Fun

IN THE OLD WEST, a surplus of whiskey often translated into an outbreak of violence. And at the White Elephant, the whiskey and the violence both flowed abundantly. The most notorious saloon in Fort Worth, Texas—and all of the western United States—its celebrity was due to the eclectic mixture of gunfighters, gamblers, and lawmen who congregated around the polished invitation of its mahogany bar. In that milieu of big wagers and strong drink, disputes were not uncommon, nor were they generally the sort that words alone could settle. And on the frigid night of February 8, 1887, one such dispute demanded that distinctly Western form of arbitration composed primarily of powder and lead. For it was on that night that, shaking with deliriem tremens and panting vapor beneath the cold light of Texas stars, a drunken former marshal and shakedown specialist named "Longhair Jim" Courtright stood outside the White Elephant and called out one of the saloon's owners, a quiet man who was known to all simply as Luke Short.

Now, the bad blood between the two may have come to

a climax on that frozen Texas eve, but fighting words most likely began two years earlier, during a high-stakes card game held at the White Elephant that included some of the most legendary names of the West, a veritable rogues' gallery of famous gunmen: The gentleman's wagers were made by none other than Wyatt Earp, Bat Masterson, Charlie Coe, and, of course, Jim Courtright and Luke Short. Courtright bailed out early, while Luke Short played extremely well and went all the way to the final hand, eventually losing with a full house to Coe's four kings. Win or lose, it was no matter—Luke's quiet confidence and ease with money irked Longhair Jim to no end. For his part, Courtright fancied himself dangerous, and rightly so—no mere gunfighting dilettante, he had accumulated numerous notches on his pistol belt for shooting down those who had stood up to him in the past. But Luke Short was no pushover, either. His mild manners and dandified demeanor disguised an experienced and exceedingly lethal gunman. Over the course of his wanderings, he had left some shallow graves of his own. Once in a quick-draw showdown at Tombstone's famous Oriental Saloon, he had, in self-defense, fired his pistol at such close range that he set his attacker's clothes on fire.

None of this seemed to deter Longhair Jim on that howling night outside the White Elephant. He ranted and raged, and demanded retribution for a gambling debt he believed Short owed him—a doubtful claim, with the real source of his acrimony more likely being Short's refusal to join his extortion racket and pay him protection money. Longhair Jim wanted satisfaction, and unlike his previous request, this was one that the mild-mannered saloon keeper happily obliged. He walked out the front door and approached the rabid Courtright, calmly insisting that he was unarmed and had no gun with which to defend himself—an obvious falsehood to anyone acquainted with the man. Courtright must not have known him well enough, though, because in the split second he took to squint and inspect Luke Short's open vest, it was already too late. That moment of hesitation sealed his own doom. With a flash fast enough to make lightning blush, Luke Short pulled his pistol and blew off Courtright's right thumb—the same thumb he required to cock back the hammer and fire his single-action revolver. As the drunken former marshal fumbled with his gun and attempted to switch hands, Luke fired four more shots into his opponent, each a one-way ticket to the grave. Longhair Jim Courtright crumpled to the ground, clothes still smoking, sputtering blood and mute curses with his gurgling last gasps.

By the law of the West, Luke Short's guilt was never in question. The murder trial that followed was merely a formality, and the verdict that came from it only made him that much more mythic. But another question does beg asking, for our humble purposes, anyway. Why did so many storied gunfighters and deathsmiths end up at the carved wooden bar of the White Elephant Saloon in the first place?

Certainly, the verdant felt of the gambling tables and lascivious winks of the sporting ladies proffered their charms. But what glinted behind its generous mahogany bar would have proven an even greater temptation to those trail-hardened and sage-scented men. For in bold, hand-stenciled letters, the establishment could state, with neither exaggeration nor boast, that it had for sale "the best brands of old sour mash whiskeys in the state." Old Crow, Old Tub, Old Forester—such names were far more familiar to thirsty cowhands than Earp, Hickok, or Holliday, and far less likely to put them in an old pine box . . . in most cases, anyway. Bourbon wasn't simply omnipresent in the Wild West—the West was genuinely wild because of it.

No Western saloon was complete without a whiskey bottle
and a card table. Seen here is Judge Roy Bean's establishment
in dusty Langtry, Texas. It's still standing today.

The Bourbon Cowboy: The West wouldn't
have been wild without its whiskey.

Whiskey was on the frontier from the very beginning, and
as that frontier expanded over the course of American history,
the range of our native liquor grew right alongside it. In the
days of George Thorpe, the "West" constituted the wilds that
lay just beyond the tidewater. For George Washington, it was
the boisterous hinterlands of western Pennsylvania. To the
Scots-Irish settlers of Kentucky and Tennessee, it was what

hid just yonder, past the cusp of their mountains. And by the final decades of the nineteenth century, with distance officially obliterated by railroads and the industrial East suddenly ravenous for new resources, the "West" became an entirely new set of territories, ones that had once belonged unambiguously to Native Americans and Mexicans, but were now freshly opened to newcomers of all sorts. Of all the cardinal directions available to Americans, one has justly received an inordinate amount of our imagination and attention. And the favored spirit of those rowdy souls who captained the compass has always been, and very likely will continue to be, whiskey.

NEVER ONE TO be outwitted, even by himself, Mark Twain offered the following nugget of wisdom on the American West:

> *How solemn and beautiful is the thought, that*
> *the earliest pioneer of civilization, the van-leader*
> *of civilization, is never the steamboat, never the*
> *railway, never the newspaper, never the Sabbath-*
> *school, never the missionary—but always whisky!*
> *Such is the case. Look history over; you will see.*
> *The missionary comes after the whisky—I mean*
> *he arrives after the whisky has arrived; next comes*
> *the poor immigrant, with ax and hoe and rifle;*
> *next, the trader; next, the miscellaneous rush;*
> *next, the gambler, the desperado, the highwayman,*
> *and all their kindred in sin of both sexes; and*
> *next, the smart chap who has bought up an old*
> *grant that covers all the land; this brings the*
> *lawyer tribe; the vigilance committee brings the*
> *undertaker. All these interests bring the newspaper;*
> *the newspaper starts up politics and a railroad;*

According to some sources, Mark Twain was as fond of
Old Crow as he was of tall tales.

all hands turn to and build a church and a jail—
and behold! civilization is established forever in
the land. But whisky, you see, was the van-leader
in this beneficent work. It always is. It was like
a foreigner—and excusable in a foreigner—to
be ignorant of this truth, and wander off into
astronomy to borrow a symbol. But if he had been
conversant with the facts, he would have said:
Westward the Jug of Empire takes its way.

How solemn and beautiful, indeed. While the passage is
certainly pat, and definitely marked by Twain's signature
hyperbole, his statement captures the essence of bourbon.
And while the foreigner Twain mentions may have confused

the anecdotal whiskey jug for a proverbial star, we are far more concerned, at least in this chapter, with "the gambler, the desperado, the highwayman" that Twain mentions just before. So let us begin. . . .

Whiskey and the West have been on intimate terms since our nation's first teetering baby steps in cowboy boots. When Lewis and Clark embarked in 1804 to explore the latter, they carried along with them ample portions of the former—six whole kegs, in fact—and even that proved inadequate. They ran out of the hard stuff at the Great Falls, and the journey that followed proved challenging without it. When the Yellowstone expedition ventured some fifteen years later into unexplored lands west of the Missouri, they were greeted by a Pawnee warrior who motioned toward his throat and playfully begged for "Whiskey, whiskey!" And we know that by 1818, the distiller Harrison Hall was labeling corn-based whiskeys produced west of the Appalachians—i.e., bourbon—"Western" whiskeys. Any fur trapper, prospector, or horse trader who alighted upon lands wild and unknown was almost certain to have some whiskey on his person, for the dual purposes of consumption and commerce. These very early encounters with the hard stuff, on the raw edge of the frontier, are what account for the amusing although not entirely accurate notion that the Western whiskey of the miners and cowboys that followed shortly thereafter was equally suitable as high-proof varnish remover. With stagecoaches and railroads still in the offing, the first whiskey to hit the frontier was more often than not rotgut, and, supply-chain issues aside, it was of such poor quality for a pretty good reason—neither the mountain men nor the Native Americans for whom it was intended were in a very good position to negotiate its quality, or demand otherwise.

The initial wave of hardscrabble and hirsute white settlers came to the West searching for beaver, buffalo, gold, and timber. And once these were procured, they immediately sought out something to drink—which brings us to the whiskey peddler, the progenitor of the legendary Western saloon. As soon as a trading post or mining camp was hacked out of the wild, a crude whiskey hall of some sort would generally accompany it. Such early saloons varied from upturned wagons to tents to simple dugouts cut into the sod. One settler described the following makeshift frontier saloon in Kansas:

> It consisted of crotched stakes . . . which supported
> a ridge-pole, across which some old sailcloth was
> drawn . . . forming a cabin some six by eight feet,
> and perhaps from three to five and a half feet
> high—large enough to contain two whiskey barrels,
> two decanters, several glasses, three or four cans of
> pickled oysters and two or three boxes of sardines
> but nothing of the bread kind whatever.

Luxurious accommodations? Hardly. And the whiskey of the West's infancy was in most cases as haphazard and bastardized as the institutions that served them. Although these drinks strove toward bourbon, and in many cases were even advertised as such, the weary frontiersman was as much a victim of false advertising as his Confederate predecessors and Gilded Age brethren back east. In the best cases, what he tossed back by the light of a tin cup lantern filled with bacon grease was foul-tasting "barrel whiskey"—the same adulterated imitation bourbon that plagued the saloons of industrial cities like New York and Philadelphia. Worst case? Well, the nauseating concoctions dreamt up by creative frontier saloonists went by names like "tanglefoot," "skull varnish," "tarantula juice," "bug juice," and "snake water," and the titles were, by most accounts, fairly accurate. An observer from the mine camp days of Arizona called the whiskey of the local tavern a "modest stock of mingled water, chemicals, and alcohol," and a few territories over, a settler described his local potation as "wretched Kansas water at five cents a glass with whiskey added to conceal the smell." A frontier traveler by the name of Irwin S. Cobb went even further in elucidating the murky "corn licker" he sampled, claiming, "It smells like gangrene starting in a mildewed silo, it tastes like the wrath to come, and when you absorb a deep swig of it you have all the sensations of having swallowed a lighted kerosene lamp." These are not the descriptions of a barrel-mellowed glass of true Kentucky sour mash, and with fair reason—prior to the introduction of stagecoaches and railroads into the frontier's untamed interior, the good stuff was a good three-month-long wagon ride away and, although delicious, not in especially strong demand in a place where men were desperate enough for a drink to drink just about anything.[*]

The first wave of white settlers may have had it tough when it came to available whiskey, but the Native Americans upon whose land they were encroaching had it significantly worse. In addition to new diseases, decimated game stocks, and befouled water sources, they also contended with the grip of the white man's "fire water." Laws against selling alcohol in Indian Country went back as far as 1802, but given the potential profits involved, such prohibitions were roundly ignored. In the 1830s, a barrel of low-quality whiskey purchased in St. Louis for as little as twenty-five cents

---

[*] It may be worth mentioning that even if a barrel of real Kentucky bourbon did make it all the way West, its contents still were not safe. It was a common trick of whiskey peddlers to slip an iron nail into the barrels of a competitor, as the whiskey would turn a repulsive shade of black if introduced to even a small amount of iron. Needless to say, drinking the stuff required an iron stomach as well.

could be worth $34 by the time it reached Fort Leavenworth in Kansas, and might sell for $64 in the Indian lands around Yellowstone.* And that single gallon of low-quality whiskey could be diluted and adulterated to make ample quantities of the befouled substance known as "Indian liquor." Just how shameful such potions were, and how shameless its merchants could be, is indicated by the following recipe as described by the frontiersman "Teddy Blue" Abbott:

> You take one barrel of Missouri River water, and
> two gallons of alcohol. Then you add two ounces
> of strychnine to make them crazy—because
> strychnine is the greatest stimulant in the world—
> and three plugs of tobacco to make them sick—an
> Indian wouldn't figure it was whisky unless it made
> him sick—and five bars of soap to give it a bead,
> and half a pound of red pepper, and then you put in
> some sagebrush and boil it until it's brown. Strain
> into a barrel, and you've got your Indian whisky;
> that one bottle calls for one buffalo robe and when
> the Indian got drunk it was two robes. And that's
> how some of the traders made their fortune.

This passage certainly does not represent one of whiskey's prouder moments, and the manner in which the spirit was used to pacify the land's native inhabitants was unquestionably deplorable. But the early West was very much a place where men with limited resources could aim to make a buck, and whether it was gold panning or whiskey peddling, fur trappers or Indian braves, bourbon whiskey, although

---

* In one appalling instance of Western whiskey inflation, an early resident of Colorado sold two measly whiskey barrels for $2,700, so great was the demand for his product, and so galling the pioneers' thirst.

On the Western frontier, the whiskey peddler was often first on the scene.

Unfortunately, frontier whiskey would play a shameful role
in subjugating Native Americans during Western expansion.

frequently contaminated and egregiously misrepresented, was present from the start.

Such was the lot of "red likker," as frontier bourbon was commonly known, in the earliest stages of Western settlement. Sold in places far removed from "civilization," it was as wild and unpredictable as the new territories in which it was sold and consumed. That all changed, however, once those remote mining camps, cattle stations, and trading posts became actual towns. All it took was a big strike, a huge cattle drive, or rumors of easy money to be made, and then the rush was on. First the wagon trains, then the railroad cars, and once a firm link to the East was in place, the dynamics of the West were altered significantly. Within months, weeks, or even days, a packed-dirt outpost at the ends of the world could transform into a real Western town. Gone were the days of tent taverns and dugouts; coming with that first holy moan of the steam engine was a whole new world, one of duded-up cowboys, bat-winged saloon doors, and high-feathered sporting ladies. A three-month wagon ride turned practically overnight into a two-day train trip, and that savage "red likker" of the fur trappers and mountain men became the same oak-aged delight savored back east.* This transformation is given voice in the following description of typical saloons in Billings, Montana:

The saloon may be a single-roomed plank cabin, neatly papered. On the walls may hang pictures of Abraham Lincoln and General Garfield, with a

---

* In most cases, anyway. Some liquor was produced and consumed locally, including the infamous "Taos Lightning" popular in the Southwest, and Utah's own "Valley Tan," which was discreetly produced by the territory's supposedly abstemious Mormons. Additionally, frontiersmen would often specifically request "sink-taller whiskey," as it was generally believed that a piece of tallow would sink in local whiskey that had been watered down.

*few comic sporting prints. A bar runs part of the
way up the room, and is spotlessly clean; behind
this counter against the wall are a few shelves
decorated with specimen-bottles of wine, spirits,
etc.; underneath, sugar, lemons, and ice, if these
luxuries are attainable; a stove, three or four chairs,
a bucket of water with a dipper, complete with
furniture.*

Wallpaper, framed pictures, diamond-dust mirrors, mahogany bars stocked with sugar and lemons—the amenities of such saloons were a far cry from the canvas-and-lumber affairs of the very first settlers; these sorts of frontier taverns were well on their way to becoming the typical Western drinking establishments that the name "saloon" conjures today. The Crystal Palace, the Oriental, and the Alhambra—three of the most famous drinking establishments in Tombstone—all were bedecked with oil paintings, mirrors, fancy brass fixtures, and richly carved mahogany bars. This was truly a saloon age, and the emergence of each new boomtown in the West was accompanied by an equally explosive increase in the number and profit potential of those slick new drinking establishments. A census taken in Sawtooth, Idaho, only a year after the camp's birth showed that of the forty-one retail stores, half were saloons; in Montana, one visitor estimated a frequency of one tavern for every eight inhabitants, and in a single year, in Leadville, Colorado, the city's 249 drinking parlors did some $4 million in business, an amount rivaled only by that generated through banking and mining itself. A business census conducted in the same town in 1879 reported ten dry-goods stores, four banks, thirty-one restaurants, and four churches. In contrast, the census recognized 120 saloons, 19 beer halls, and 228 gambling houses and private-club rooms—an economic and social landscape undeniably skewed in favor of the drinking class.

Obviously, the primary attraction for any saloon keeper was financial. But there was more to bar backing than simply making a buck. In the Western town or frontier outpost, the saloon keeper held a unique and respectable position as the overseer of what amounted to the only significant source of entertainment or refreshment around. He was in many cases a genuine pillar of the community, as noted again by an observant Mark Twain:

> The cheapest and easiest way to become an influential man and be looked up to by the community at large, was to stand behind a bar, wear a cluster-diamond pin, and sell whiskey. I am not sure but that the saloon-keeper held a shade higher rank than any other member of society. . . . No great movement could succeed without the countenance and direction of the saloon-keeper.

When the cowpunchers and gamblers rolled in, the saloon keeper was an honest and straightforward man they could generally count on to serve them a much-needed drink at a fair rate. Not the greatest of feats perhaps, creating that small bit of hospitality in an inhospitable place, but still a necessary one, and for that alone he evidently was highly esteemed.

And what drink, pray tell, did all these roughriders and gold miners order when they slapped their two bits on the freshly polished bar, shipped in pieces by train from manufactures back east? Why, bourbon whiskey, of course. Favorite brands included Old Crow, Old Tub, Old Pepper, Old Gideon, Old Anderson's Little Brown Jug, Old Hermitage, and Clarke's. Some hotels and saloons, like the Grand Central in Denver and the Oriental in

Tombstone, even sold their own brands of bourbon to their customers, labeled as such. Consumption among the rambunctious clientele was heavy—in the Dakotas, one estimate put the average intake for a cowhand or miner at five tumblers a day. Other estimates have it at a gallon of whiskey per week, and plenty of bar tabs from Montana and the Dakotas from the 1880s and 1890s show that benders consisting of "thirty slugs per diem" were not uncommon.* Prices for a single drink ranged from ten cents for a glass of the cheap barrelhouse bourbon† from St. Louis or Cincinnati to as much as fifty cents a glass for the good stuff from Kentucky. And any time a gambler hit it big in a game of faro, a miner struck a promising load just outside of town, or a cowboy received his trail bonus after a long month on the range, you can be sure he was ordering the good stuff for himself and his compadres.

Saloons may have served the bulk of the bourbon, but they were not the only places in a Western town where the whiskey flowed freely. Hurdy-gurdy dance halls, variety theaters, and good old-fashioned brothels were all locales where a man of the range, if so inclined, could enjoy the comforts of whiskey while ogling the delights of the flesh. Hurdy-gurdy and variety halls were essentially the strip clubs of their day—at the sec-

---

* Speaking of benders, Mark Twain and three of his buddies once ran up a bar tab in Virginia City, Nevada, of $237, in an era when a good drink cost fifty cents. Twain's friend Artemus Ward proposed a standing toast toward its conclusion, only to realize that he was the only one who could stand. Given Western drinking habits, we must grant them some Clemens-y.

† This cheaper "bourbon" would have been, in most cases, the very same class of blended midwestern corn whiskey that the Whiskey Trust was mass-producing in the Gilded Age, and that the Kentucky distillers were attempting to differentiate themselves from. Both, as it were, turned out to be big hits in the West.

The good stuff at last: Bourbon heads west on the Sour Mash Express.

ond, scantily clad women "pole-danced" the cancan, and at the first, men could earn a waltz with a young woman by buying drinks at the bar. Although this was not quite the modern champagne room, the dancers did receive a commission on drinks the men purchased, and said drinks usually consisted of good bourbon for him and diluted champagne for her. Naturally, with liquor and vigorous dancing, scandalous behavior was never far behind, a reality best demonstrated by the dancer Grace Carlyle's evening at Crumley's drinking establishment in Cripple Creek, Colorado. After copious alcohol consumption, the night ended with the platinum blond mademoiselle being hoisted on the bar to gyrate naked—all to the wild applause of the men in attendance. The *Cripple Creek Crusher* would later explain away the incident, stating:

> *Such hilarious antics were nothing more than an expression of the natural ebullience of the world's*

richest mining camp and the increased potency of
good Bourbon at high altitudes and not to be taken
as proof of the town's depravity.

Good bourbon at high altitudes—an adequate excuse, no doubt, for many such immodest dance hall displays. As for the brothels, what occurred there may be better fodder for a father-to-son chat or a junior high health class than a bourbon history, but we can rest assured that a bottle of bourbon was equally complicit in more than a few of the many dalliances they facilitated.*

Taking a step back, and examining the various elements that congregated in a typical Western town, a combustible truth emerges. Whiskey, women, gambling—such elements are volatile in almost any environment, but enlist for their combined enjoyment a class of gun-handy, exceptionally proud men bound only by the weakest inklings of organized law, and you've got a recipe for, well . . . some of the most rootin', tootin' gunfights in the West. Tender a quick run-down of the most famous of such standoffs, and it becomes clear that saloons served as the setting for a disproportion-ately large number. This ought to come as no surprise to any-one who has seen a cowboy movie, or simply observed what happens in a bar when two drunk guys get into an argument over whose turn it is at the pool table. The saloons of the Wild West served as the ideal incubator of frontier conflicts, and the perfect stage for the all-American gunfight. For contrary to what some revisionist histories might tell you, the West truly was an incredibly violent place. With many Civil War veterans

---

* According to legend, the term "red-light district" has its origins in Dodge City, where brakemen from the railroads would leave their red lanterns hanging outside the doors of their, ahem, sweethearts' chambers. If that's not true, it should be.

holding on to their service weapons, not to mention the new Colt revolvers and Winchester rifles being turned out by the thousands, guns were plentiful and shootouts not uncommon. At least one tally estimates that between 1866 and 1900, as many as twenty thousand Westerners were killed by gunshot. And in a tremendous number of those killings, bourbon whiskey, either true Kentucky or a cheaper variant, proved to be the oil in the gun chambers.

Just how wild could things get when the cowboys rode and the whiskey flowed? Well, if the exploits of the legendary Jim Lafer, who was wanted dead or alive for murder in both Arizona and New Mexico, are any example, wild indeed. Just take a look-see at what the *Las Vegas Optic* wrote about the carousing villain in 1888:

> *In Loma Parda, James Lafer is still remembered as the man who picked up a New Mexican woman in the street, placed her across his horse in front of him and rode into a saloon, making the bartender set up drinks for the whole party. And because his horse would not drink, he shot him through the head, lifted the woman from the saddle before the horse fell, and walked out, leaving the dead horse lying on the floor.*

Shocking, yes, the misdeeds of men like James Lafer, although admittedly atypical; the vast majority of violence in the West was not enacted by the famous gunslingers and notorious villains who continue to capture our imaginations to this day. Most of the gunplay that transpired was a result of the same pedestrian species of conflict one encounters anywhere where liquor and testosterone mingle too freely. In other words, just regular bar fights involving regular Joes who'd had way too much to drink. Between March and October of 1880, in Leadville, Colorado, alcohol was involved in at least half of the fourteen murders recorded during that period. And of those fourteen killings, three were caused by debt disputes, either gambling or otherwise, four were provoked by jealousies of the sexual variety, and the remaining seven were the result of pure madness or heat-of-the-moment rage. The case of a Billie Wall, from Creede, Colorado, serves as a fine example of what may be classified under the last category. Upon departing Grayman's Saloon in a drunken state on April 1, 1892, Mr. Wall found it necessary to crouch over the gutter and expel the contents of his whiskey-laden stomach. "Puke, you son of a bitch!" a nearby drunk taunted him. Billie Wall took a break from his vomiting long enough to reply in kind, at which point his equally inebriated antagonist pulled a pistol instead and relieved Billie of his life. The newspapers of the day, in boomtowns scattered across the West, carried similar tales of debauchery and gunplay, with a frequency that both horrified and fascinated those "civilized" and "cultured" citizens back east.

What interested the Eastern city slickers far more, however, than the drunken shenanigans of bumbling miners or besotted cowpokes were the less common although no less real exploits of the West's most celebrated gunmen. And the same bourbon whiskey that doomed poor Billie Wall was equally culpable in their highly publicized gun duels. A quick tally of the places said duels took place will reveal just how central the saloon was to the culture of masculine violence that permeated the West, and to the far larger body of Western life as a whole. Where does one begin? Well, order up a shot of bourbon, pull up a chair, and let's see who gets dealt the deadman's hand in the Wild West poker game of fate. . . .

Why not start with the crowd-pleaser, John Henry "Doc"

Make 'em dance: When the whiskey flowed, saloons often turned rowdy.

Holliday, a man that gunfighter Bat Masterson* would describe years later as "unable to keep out of trouble" yet "more often in the right than in the wrong," and whom Wyatt Earp would call the "nerviest, speediest, deadliest man with a six-gun" he had ever seen. When extracting teeth in Dallas proved less profitable than gambling, the good doctor hung up his molar-shaped shingle and toured the wildest outposts of the frontier, killing an opponent in a saloon brawl near Fort Richardson, dealing faro at the Bella Union saloon in Cheyenne and later Deadwood, knifing to death another man following a drunken gambling dispute in Fort Griffin, and hooting it up with his drinking buddy Wyatt Earp in every spirits parlor between Dodge City and Tombstone—the two men had become lifelong friends when Doc scared off a rowdy bunch of trigger-happy cowboys out to get Wyatt in a Kansas saloon. Doc's final gun duel would be fought in Leadville's Monarch Saloon, where on a hot August night in 1884, a deplorably naive local by the name of Bill Allen thought busting into the Monarch and threatening Doc Holliday with a gun would convince him to pay back the $5 he owed him. The plan backfired, but Doc's single-action .45 revolver did not—it blew a hole through Allen's arm and ended his debt-collecting days for good. It's impossible to know exactly how many shortsighted or ill-advised desperadoes were dealt angel's wings by Holliday's pistol, but some estimates put the total at more than thirty. Gross exaggeration or not, the two constants that accompanied the courtly Southern dentist during his career as a gunfighter were the tuberculosis that would eventually end his days, and the whiskey he used to ease

---

* Unlike many gunfighters, Bat Masterson actually lived to reach old age, leaving the West and becoming a well-known sportswriter in New York City, where he regaled friends with tales of the Old West until his death in 1921. And unlike most gunfighters, Bat wasn't American—he was among the West's most famous Canucks.

his suffering. In fact, on his deathbed, unable to fend off the disease any longer, the thirty-six-year-old Holliday made his final request, for a glass of whiskey, shortly before gazing down at his bootless feet and observing, "Damn, this is funny." Whether it was the whiskey, his socks, or the absurdity of death that provoked the comment, we will never know. Those words were his last.

Among the mourners was of course Doc's old friend Wyatt Earp, a saloon keeper, gambler, and deputy marshal who was widely regarded as the toughest lawman of the West.* He shot it out with drunken cowboys in Dodge City, pistol-whipped an intoxicated gun-toting reveler in Tombstone, and took up partial ownership of a faro game at the notorious Oriental Saloon. Although Earp would settle and buy into saloons in towns across the West, it was in Tombstone on October 26, 1881, that his most famous altercation took place—the Gunfight at the O.K. Corral—a dispute first kicked up in the smoky saloon taprooms of the Alhambra and Grand hotels, when the local lawmen began accusing some rambunctious cowboys of lying and thievery. In fact, Wyatt's brother, Virgil, would smuggle a double-barreled shotgun into another nearby saloon called Hafford's, for the use of the assembled posse of lawmen, with its contents to be unloaded shortly thereafter in a most insalubrious fashion upon their cowboy foes, Messieurs Clanton and McLaury. The entire battle may have lasted only thirty seconds, but its legend has endured, and without the bourbon-dealing saloons of Tombstone, it never would have happened.

---

* Lest anyone take Wyatt Earp for too law-abiding a citizen, it deserves mention that he was arrested and charged on numerous occasions for a variety of offenses, and aside from an early career in Illinois as very likely a pimp, he was also forced to pay a $1 fine in Dodge City for slapping a particularly muscular prostitute by the name of Frankie Bell. Oh, and he killed a lot of people, too.

Happy hour wasn't always that happy at Dodge City's Long
Branch Saloon . . . and high noon was even worse.

Naturally, no mention of Doc Holliday and Wyatt Earp
would be complete without including their old haunt the Long
Branch Saloon. And no mention of the Long Branch could be
judged adequate without invoking the names of its two most
infamous patrons, Levi Richardson and Frank Loving. Their
destinies crossed paths beneath the Long Branch's amber
whiskey bottles and sprawling moose antlers on the evening of
April 5, 1879, when the two men discovered their mutual
affection for a local Dodge City dance hall girl. Levi had concluded a long night of whiskey drinking and was on his way
out the door when destiny pushed Frank past him on his way
in. Some unkind words were exchanged, ones shortly to
become of the fighting variety, and in short order Richardson
reached under his coat and pulled his piece. Loving wasn't far
behind, and when the two drawn muzzles faced each other,
they were nearly close enough to touch. Richardson must have
had about ten whiskeys too many, because the two shots he
squeezed off at point-blank range thudded harmlessly into the

wall. Whatever advantage Loving had in sobriety was soon lost to a severe shortage in the luck department—his pistol misfired, the hammer snapping down on a defective bullet. Realizing his misfortune, Loving leapt up on a billiard table while the bourbon-dazed Richardson fired and missed twice more, the errant shots filling the air with splinters and hot cordite. In the haze and confusion of gun smoke, Loving was able to once again attempt a shot, and this time with far better results, blasting off two rounds that sent Richardson diving behind a cast-iron stove. From his perch behind its potbelly, he returned fire. Loving did fall to the floor, but from slipping on spilled whiskey, not from a wound; the bullet zinged harmlessly by him. A bystander, thinking the fallen Loving to be grievously wounded, snatched the gun from Richardson's hand, intending to keep it a fair fight. Little did he know that Loving was alive and well and still holding securely on to his six-shooter. He got up, aimed carefully, and got off three rounds . . . all three of which ripped into Levi Richardson's cowering form and scared the ghost plumb out of him. The gods of the West smiled on Frank Loving that night, but his luck was not to last—three years later, he got his, at a gunfight in Trinidad, Colorado.

Frontier misfortune of this kind was endemic to the whiskey-soaked world of the Western saloon. Few figures embodied the era better than the gunfighter and lawman Wild Bill Hickok.* His pistol battles were the stuff of legend—he is credited with inventing the classic Western quick-draw duel, and won showdowns in saloons through-

---

* Perhaps the most amusing incident of Wild Bill's career as a lawman took place in Abilene, where he very nearly had it out with Phil Coe for refusing to remove a painting of a bull's penis from the side of his tavern. Bill got some paint and removed it himself, and very nearly started a war in the process. No bull.

out the West. Yet his last confrontation was anything but heroic. As fond of gambling and drinking as he was of gunplay, Wild Bill met his end at one of his many poker games at Nuttal & Mann's Saloon in Deadwood, Dakota Territory, where he was forced for a lack of chairs to sit with his back to the door—something the veteran gunman usually avoided, and with good reason. As Wild Bill sipped his whiskey and studied his hand, a disgruntled gambler and buffalo hunter named Jack McCall snuck up behind him and blew his brains out, ending in one pull of a trigger the life and career of one of the Old West's most compelling and genuinely lethal characters. The two aces and two eights that Hickok was holding when the fatal shot was fired have come to be known as the deadman's hand, in honor of the hard-drinking, hard-gambling, hard-fighting Wild Bill Hickok.

Doc Holliday, Wyatt Earp, Frank Loving, and Wild Bill Hickok may be among the more notable of the Western whiskey drinkers and gunfighters, but they were hardly alone in their saloon-based exploits. Billy the Kid killed his first man at George Adkins' Saloon in the Arizona Territory; the marshal Mike Meagher swallowed his share of lead in an outhouse next to Hope's Saloon in Wichita, but still came out blasting and won the day. John Wesley Hardin, after a lifetime of infamy, got it good at the Acme Saloon in old El Paso, and Robert Ford, a despised barkeep known only for adulterating his own whiskey and having murdered Jesse James, came upon an equally gruesome fate in a Colorado tavern known as the Creede Exchange—his throat was ripped to shreds by two barrels of buckshot and one very angry customer. These men were all whiskey drinkers, all gunfighters, and they contributed to a mythic conception of the West that lived far longer than they did. Even to this day, if you walk into the right old saloon and know where to look, you can find bullet holes still notched into the walls, a reminder of what happened when the bourbon flowed a little too copiously, and ran headlong into the violent code of the American West.

FOR THE CLASS of gamblers, gunmen, desperadoes, and buckaroos that elevated the settlement of the West into a national mythology complete with its own pantheon of gun-slinging immortals, the lawlessness of that time and place was precisely what enabled their aggrandized lifestyle. But, as the old adage proclaims, all good things must come to an end. The Old or Wild West lasted from the end of the Civil War roughly until the close of the nineteenth century, and in a few especially rough-and-tumble places it persisted a bit longer. By the early twentieth century, however, it was clear that an era had passed, and just as Mark Twain's "jug of empire" so astutely predicted, "civilization," with all of its connotations of order, decency, and regulation, had perme-ated and conquered the once wild lands of the Western fron-tier. By 1892, one observer noted that "the coming of the barb-wire fence and the railroad killed the cowboy as a pic-turesque element of the recklessness and lawlessness. . . . It suppressed him and localized him to his own range, and made his revolver merely an ornament." And as it pertained to their drink of choice, the Texas historian Owen White, who had witnessed the Wild West as a child in El Paso dur-ing the 1880s, lamented half a century later:

> *Those fine old-timers who used to come to town*
> *for a hell of a time, and have it when they got there,*
> *who played poker, monte, and faro bank with*
> *the far and beautiful North Star as the limit, who*
> *took cold unless they carried a six-shooter and a*

Winchester, who slept better on the ground than
they did on a mattress, who "rolled their own" and
drank whiskey out of tin drippers have now entirely
disappeared from the face of Texas.

True, by the dawn of the 1900s, the sun had set on the age of the Old West. But the spirit of the West, in terms of both the ethanol and the ethereal, remained. And the experience of settling the West—Manifest Destiny, imperial expansion, conquest, call it what you will—had a profound and lasting effect upon the character of our nation, and paved the way, almost literally, for the twentieth century and the modern era.

How so? Frederick Jackson Turner and his pithy frontier thesis aside, there are the obvious ways that still warrant mention. Naturally, new population centers out west meant new and thirsty markets; the end of Western expansion meant that America could start to turn its attention and its imperialistic ambitions outward, to take a new and more active role in world affairs, particularly those that were starting to roil Europe as some of those older empires began to unravel. And there was the dramatic increase in cultivated farmland in the new Western lands, in a region particularly hospitable to corn. Between 1870 and 1900 the number of American farms rose from 2.6 million to 5.7 million, with acreage jumping from 408 million to 841 million. Most of this expansion occurred on the Great Plains, grasslands whose richness had formerly nourished vast herds of the now vanished bison and the Native Americans whose survival depended on them. In Kansas, Nebraska, and the Dakotas alone, the 50,000 existing farms had ballooned to nearly 400,000 by the end of the century; the tremendous influx of corn into the market only dropped the price of the grain further, boosting bourbon way ahead of America's other and more eastern-leaning whiskey, rye.*

As for other developments, well, by the early 1900s, a new kind of music was spreading out of the African-American juke joints of St. Louis and New Orleans, destined to sweep across the saloons and dance halls of the West. It was known as "ragtime," and although it could readily be tinkled out on those same old barroom ivories, it had a decidedly modern, almost "jazzy" feel. To accompany those snappy new melodies, a fresh way to imbibe was also taking hold, perhaps spawned initially by the low-quality liquor served in early frontier taverns. Known as "cocktails," these mixed drinks varied from the highfalutin martinis first served in San Francisco to the simple boilermakers concocted in Butte, Montana. And lastly, in towns across the West, the mild-mannered temperance movement that had existed since the days of George Washington was steadily gaining steam thanks to a cantankerous, six-foot-tall harridan by the name of Carrie Nation. She was born in Kentucky, deep in bourbon country, but just like bourbon, she had made her way west. And luckily for an ambitious young thug by the name of Alphonse Capone, she brought her hatchet and her zeal for Prohibition along with her.

Are you ready for the twentieth century? Because bourbon sure is. The American Spirit is oiling its tommy gun, limbering up to do the Charleston, and preparing for what will prove to be the most dramatic, colorful, and explosive period since the corn first met the still—and if the gangsters don't getcha, there are flappers sitting barside who almost certainly will.

---

* Although corn-based bourbon dominated the West, there were among those frontiersmen some who still carried a taste for rye. Doc Holliday was said to enjoy a glass of Old Overholt when he could get it, and Buffalo Bill Cody was said to take his rye mixed with apple cider. Not the manliest of cocktails, but you wouldn't want to let Bill hear you say that.

7

An Irishman, an Italian, a Pole Walk into a Bar . . . and Prohibition Begins

THE TWENTIES WERE justly famous for their wild parties, but the lavishness and pure decadence of the soiree that took place one sultry July evening in 1923 put them all to inglorious shame. It was staged outside a palatial mansion, just beyond the reach of city lights; its attendees included an eclectic mix of debutantes, society people, celebrities, and wannabes. These glittering guests, once assembled, cavorted and sipped cocktails as the summer night ripened before them, the succulent murmur of their conversations punctuated at steady intervals by the popping of champagne corks and the richness of feminine laughter. Emboldened perhaps by the effervescence of the champagne, they took to exploring the manicured gardens, stables of Thoroughbreds, and fountain-fed swimming pools that encircled the mansion, discovering at the latter a fifteen-piece orchestra accompanying a water ballet, choreographed and performed just for the occasion. To sweeten the mood even further, party favors were graciously handed out by tuxedoed butlers, a jeweled ring for each female guest, and a diamond tie clasp for every male. The gasps that were uttered upon their reception were drowned out shortly thereafter by the cries of amazement as the first of the attendees began to depart—upon leaving the fete, they were presented with their own brand-new 1923 Pontiac from a cavalcade of the automobiles gleaming on the driveway. How was it possible? How could it be? Gossip flourished among the glow of paper lanterns and the chiming of cocktail glasses, most of which concerned the mysterious host, who was nowhere to be found. A group of more adventurous revelers entered the dark coolness of the mansion proper, intent on finding this peculiar, enigmatic man, and find him they did—sitting quietly and alone in his library, reading a book and enjoying, with a wonderment on his face that bordered on boyish, the pleasant sounds coming in from the spectacle he had created. . . .

"Whoa, whoa, whoa," the mildly incredulous and literature-loving reader is by this point almost certainly exclaiming. "This is a history of bourbon, and what you're describing is a chapter from *The Great Gatsby*." A fair point, if only it were true. For while the scene above mirrors that which F. Scott Fitzgerald captured so beautifully in purplish prose, the man in question is not Jay Gatsby—although his very real exploits almost certainly inspired Fitzgerald. His name was George Remus, and just like his fictional counterpart, he threw elaborate parties, courted high society, and desperately wanted to shed the taint of his working-class, immigrant past. And, just like Gatsby, his staggering fortune was founded on crime; beneath his facade of credibility, he was little more than a bootlegger, and the source of his wealth was bourbon whiskey.

So how did he do it? Well, when a cultural staple like

alcohol was declared illegal, there was suddenly no end to the amount of money to be made in ensuring its availability. Through a combination of intelligence, shrewdness, and occasional ruthlessness, men such as George Remus were able to capitalize on its prohibition to generate tremendous amounts of wealth, in a manner hardly different from the Pablo Escobars of more recent times. The case of Mr. Remus is especially interesting because he was able to conduct so much of his business right out in the open, with the fruits of his illicit labor on such prominent display. For unlike many of his bootlegging peers, George was not a disenfranchised hood from an ethnic ghetto, but a criminal defense lawyer with a background in pharmaceuticals—the perfect résumé, as it turned out, for becoming a successful bootlegger. From his courtroom days in Chicago, he had built up a network of useful contacts that included names like Johnny Torrio and Al Capone. And thanks to his experience behind the pharmacy counter, he was well aware of the prescription loophole that allowed for the sale of "medicinal" whiskey. These two credentials, when combined, offered a legal way to procure the whiskey, and a highly illegal way to move it out the back door and traffic it to thirsty customers.

All that remained for George Remus was to find the source for his liquor, which led him naturally in the direction of America's whiskey-pumping Kentucky heart. A visionary in a myopic age, George Remus wasted no time in relocating from Chicago to Cincinnati, on the very edge of bourbon country, where millions of gallons of sour mash whiskey were resting untapped in government-controlled warehouses. Thusly situated, he then proceeded to scoop up at a discounted price the nearly bankrupt distilleries and their vast stocks of padlocked whiskey and funnel their output through a series of false-front drug companies he opened all over the city. Once those ostensibly "legal" distributors were estab-

Remains of a borrowed stutz touring
car after running into a tree at a
speed of seventy miles an hour, in
which the bootlegger driver was kill

Delivery gone bad: A bootlegger's car wrecked
while transporting illegal alcohol during Prohibition.

lished, and a few legitimate medicinal bottles were positioned
on the shelves, it was simply a question of bribery and creative
accounting to make sure most of his bourbon whiskey was
sold under the table to his underworld acquaintances, who,
with considerable assistance from tommy guns and ominous
fedoras, channeled it directly to illegal speakeasies across
America. It was beautiful in its simplicity, the bourbon scheme
of George Remus, and as with his literary counterpart, Jay
Gatsby, it turned him very quickly into a very rich man.*

As compelling a task as divining the source of the Great

---

* Also like Gatsby, George Remus's meteoric rise resulted in a lethal love
triangle; the bootlegger killed his wife after discovering her affair with
one of the very Prohibition agents who had been after him. In a sign of the

Remus's wealth is, an even more relevant one for our purposes is determining the source of the laws that enabled it. Because despite popular misconceptions, Prohibition was not a rash gubernatorial decision or a decade-long case of mass hysteria, but rather the culmination of a nativist backlash that had been mounting for years. The Volstead Act had many champions and far-flung fathers, but at its core, it was the legal expression of a shared discomfort, a general rejection of the very tides that were transforming America into a modern, progressive, and multicultural society. And as is the case with all things authored by those with limited vision, the foresight it lacked would prove disastrous for their cause. Far from the mild-mannered and churchgoing era that the Anti-Saloon League envisioned, the crusade against alcohol gave birth instead to flappers, gangsters, Hemingway, and Hollywood—contributors all to a spirit of flamboyant creativity that would redefine the American Spirit for a new American century.

Want to hear more? There's a blind tiger just down the alley where you can dip the bill with some real tomatoes. Put on your glad rags and pack some iron, 'cause this ain't no common gin mill. There's a reason they call them the Roaring Twenties, and illegal bourbon—known as "corn" down at the speakeasy—is going to provide much of their gusto.

ALCOHOL AND AMERICA have been inseparable companions since the days of George Thorpe—even long before that, if you consider the drinking habits of indigenous Mesoamericans. As we have seen, the first explorers drank, the

---

times, he received no jail time for the murder, although he did serve two years for illegally selling alcohol.

A government agent gives booze the ax, 1924.

Founding Fathers drank, the earliest pioneers drank, and even when the nation came close to tearing itself apart, it still managed to sneak in some healthy swigs from its hip flask. Yet despite all this, by the first decade of the twentieth century, alcohol had come to represent for many Americans all that was foreign, unknown, and irreconcilably different. As to how this came to pass, just about anything is possible when shifts in demographics upset the status quo, and that's exactly what was happening during the painful adolescence of our modern nation. For the first two centuries or so of its existence, America had been a predominantly agrarian and Protestant society, the obvious legacy of British colonization and settlement. After half a century of fresh immigration, however, from countries neither Anglo nor Saxon, the cultural, economic, and political hegemony that small-town America had long taken for granted was beginning to unravel. Beginning with the first wave of Irish Catholic refugees fleeing the Potato Famine in the mid-nineteenth century, and continuing into the twentieth with successive waves of Germans, Italians, and Eastern Europeans, the cultural landscape of the United States was rapidly changing, particularly in its eastern and midwestern cities, where industrial jobs were ripe for the picking. A bustling new version of the American dream was taking form in these cosmopolitan melting pots, with hyphenated yet uniquely American identities congealing alongside it.

To understand how alcohol figures into the country's changing cityscape, it is crucial to examine the establishment in which it was served: the urban saloon. Found generally in poor neighborhoods that could claim few meaningful social clubs, news agencies, sporting complexes, or political offices, the local saloon provided all of those multifarious services to the immigrant underclass. They were crucial to the social and political life of urban communities, and they were in many cases owned by immigrants themselves. As early as the 1880s, a Daniel Dorchester noted that "the names over the saloons, beer gardens and low groceries are mostly foreign," a fact that would become only more apparent over the next several decades, particularly to those with nativist tendencies and political ambitions of their own. The Anti-Saloon League was not the nail in the publican's coffin in and of itself; but when its cause began to align with those of such varied interests as the suffrage movement, who sought to keep men from spending family wages on liquor, and the Ku Klux Klan, whose nonsensical disdain for Catholics and Jews nearly rivaled that which they harbored for blacks, the movement really became a force to be reckoned with. And in regions where such interests held considerable sway, ensuring the demise of ethnic saloons—the Irish pub, the German beer hall, the Italian wineshop—became a top priority. Carrie Nation may have lent to the cause much of its fanaticism and zeal, but the real edge on its hatchet was the mounting distrust among rural, native-born Americans toward the burgeoning new world of our multicultural cities.

The transformation of alcohol from a ubiquitous intoxicant into a controlled substance did not happen instantaneously, nor was it the result of any one event or action. By 1903 as much as one-third of the country possessed state or local laws banning its consumption; a decade later, that fraction would climb to half, with the South and the Midwest leading the charge. When anti-German sentiment reached its zenith during World War I, passing a wartime ban on alcohol production proved to be a cinch. Wayne Wheeler, the political power broker behind the increasingly powerful Anti-Saloon League, would demand that government officials investigate the "alien enemies" who controlled such innocuous household

"In the Name of God and Humanity": Prohibition's backers believed they were part of a noble crusade to rid the country of vice—they couldn't have been more wrong.

names as Anheuser-Busch. By the time the Volstead Act was ratified by the necessary thirty-six states in 1919, the idea of a national prohibition on alcohol was an inevitable and unfortunate reality.

Still, while the American people may have seen Prohibi-

tion coming from a long way off,* that doesn't mean everybody knew exactly what to do when the new Eighteenth
Amendment became law on January 17, 1920. The day before
Prohibition officially came into effect, the *Daily News* released
the following useful tips for perplexed New Yorkers:

> *You may drink intoxicating liquor in your own
> home or in the home of a friend when you are a
> bona fide guest.*
> *You may buy intoxicating liquor on a bona fide
> medical prescription of a doctor. A pint can be
> bought every ten days.*
> *You may consider any place you live permanently
> as your home. If you have more than one home, you
> may keep a stock of liquor in each.*
> *You may keep liquor in any storage room or club
> locker, provided the storage place is for the exclusive
> use of yourself, family, or bona fide friends.*
> *You may get a permit to move liquor when you
> change your residence.*
> *You may manufacture, sell or transport liquor for
> non-beverage or sacramental purposes provided
> you obtain a Government permit.*
> *You cannot carry a hip flask.*
> *You cannot give away or receive a bottle of liquor
> as a gift.*
> *You cannot take liquor to hotels or restaurants and
> drink it in the public dining rooms.*
> *You cannot buy or sell formulas or recipes for
> homemade liquors.*

---

* It's no coincidence that the first federal income tax was implemented in
1913—it was intended to compensate for the loss of alcohol revenues that
at that point already seemed inevitable . . . and proof that the folks at the
IRS were as much of a pain in the keister then as they are today.

You cannot ship liquor for beverage use.
You cannot manufacture anything above one half
of one percent (liquor strength) in your home.
You cannot store liquor in any place except your
own home.
You cannot display liquor signs or advertisements
on your premises.
You cannot reserve stocks from storage.

Needless to say, it was a lot to take in. And while average citizens and bourbon distillers alike scratched their heads and tried to make sense of it, the first harbingers of what was to come were already dusting off their knuckle-dusters and practicing their most menacing leers. The same day popular evangelists like Billy Sunday claimed that "the reign of tears is over," and "hell will be forever for rent," a few tough Chicago boys with very different notions of paradise decided to make their mark. Within only an hour of the Volstead Act's having taken effect, six masked and armed men held up a medicinal whiskey supplier and made off with $100,000 worth of doctor-approved bourbon. Hell very well may have been up for rent, but as America was soon to find out, men willing to pay that fee were all but legion.

But back to the business of drinking, and the more exigent question of how to keep the booze flowing in a country that had ostensibly gone dry. Prohibition may have hampered alcohol's availability, but it didn't do much to alter America's thirst. And just as everyday citizens quickly came around to the ideas of underground speakeasies and bathtub gin, the bourbon industry, too, required resourcefulness and creativity to keep the stills running . . . or at the very least, from being sold for copper scrap. The wealthiest and most perspicacious distillers had scrambled to ship vast quantities of bourbon outside U.S. borders in the frantic

Forward-thinking Americans stocked up on
bourbon before the Volstead Act took effect.

days before Prohibition became law. The most famous of
such shipments was that of the 4,125-ton freighter the *Lake
Ellerslie*, which steamed out of Baltimore the same day that
Prohibition kicked in, destined for the Bahamas, laden with
almost half a million bottles' worth of whiskey and wine.
The Hill & Hill distillery alone would ship sixty thousand
bottles of Kentucky bourbon to the islands, helping to turn
them into America's offshore liquor store—at least for any
rumrunner bold enough to try it.* For the majority of bour-

---

* The most famous of the period's rumrunners was the former navy
first mate Bill McCoy. His vessel *Arethusa* was known for both its
beauty and its deadliness—the deck bristled with a swiveling machine-
gun emplacement on prominent display for any would-be hijackers. His
success in smuggling high-quality whiskey off the islands would make him
famous . . . and give birth to the expression "the real McCoy."

bon distillers, however, such forms of adventuring were simply not an option. Somehow or another, bourbon had to find a way to stay afloat during a time when the Constitution itself was dead-set on sinking it; lucky for all of us, whiskey is less dense than water, and the American Spirit not so easily foundered.

The dilemma bourbon distilleries faced was two pronged: First and foremost, they wanted to stay in business and continue distilling whiskey, but second, and perhaps less intuitively, they had to figure out a way to unload their massive quantities of aging stock. The realities of the bourbon-making process dictated that at any given moment, a tremendous proportion of a distillery's net worth would be tied up—or barreled up, more accurately—in an aging warehouse, where it would remain for anywhere between five and ten years. All of which meant that when Prohibition came into effect, Kentucky's traditional bourbon distilleries suddenly had huge chunks of liquid capital held under lock and key by the federal government. And getting to those barrels and unloading them into the market became just as much a priority as keeping a fire under the still.

For a fortunate few, existing stocks and production stocks of bourbon whiskey were able to be sold during Prohibition as medicinal whiskey. Taking their cue from men like George Remus, those distillers with the funds and connections could obtain a license to continue producing and selling bourbon. The American Medical Association, after only two years of Prohibition, officially reversed its previous stance and fully endorsed alcohol as a form of medication. There was suddenly a fortune to be made in the medicinal whiskey industry, and anyone who could benefit from it did.

This included the bourbon makers who were able to get their hands on one of the much-coveted permits issued

Contraband whiskey recovered from smugglers was often
destroyed in bulk, much to the dismay of thirsty Americans.

by the government. Most prominent among them were the
Wathen brothers of Louisville, makers of Old Grand-Dad
bourbon whiskey. Seeing opportunity at hand, they reor-
ganized their corporation and renamed it the American
Medicinal Spirits Company, eventually gathering fifty-eight
additional brands under that name (distillers without a per-

mit were understandably desperate to sell out). The final barrel-aged product was essentially unchanged, although the bottle labels began to carry the now improbably hilarious message "Unexcelled for Medicinal Purposes." Another distiller to take advantage of the medicinal movement was the Brown-Forman company, who, as you may recall, had been marketing its Old Forester whiskey to pharmacies since its inception. While many distillers were forced to sell or go under, Brown-Forman was able to send off a train bearing a dozen armed guards and 6,750 gallons of its bourbon to a Boston druggist confident he could resell it in the form of 54,000 legal-sized medicinal pints. The firm's acquisition of the entire existing stock of the Early Times bourbon label ensured that it wouldn't even need to make more whiskey to fill its fast-flowing orders. All that was required by law for a regular American citizen to obtain medicinal whiskey was a doctor's note, a mandate that one Detroit physician answered with the charmingly trite prescription "Take three ounces every hour for stimulant until stimulated." It was a prescription that the makers of medical bourbon were eager to fill.

Unfortunately for the bulk of bourbon makers, fewer than a dozen medicinal permits were ever issued, and the brands that got in on the action early cornered the market in no time at all. And although some government-controlled stocks could be sold off to the licensed medicinal providers, those stubborn distillers who were left in the cold but unwilling to give up were forced to find a new means to stay in business. For some, this meant trying out new business ventures. The venerable Chicken Cock distillery became a temporary seed company. Rolling Fork put up some fences and transformed into a stockyard. The Beam family, dispossessed of their ancestral livelihood, started the Sunlight Mining Company and Sunbeam Quarries

Prescription whiskey: A bourbon a day keeps the doctor
away . . . until it's time for a refill.

Company, as well as a citrus farm in Florida, none of which
did particularly well.

Among the traditional distilling class of Kentucky and
Tennessee, a few brave souls refused to kneel before Prohibition, and instead took their cue from the Will Rogers
mantra "Prohibition is better than no liquor at all." Bourbon whiskey had always been a custodian of sorts for the
more rebellious and rabble-rousing facets of the American
Spirit, and that spirit's flame was not extinguished by the
passing of the Eighteenth Amendment. There were some
who chose to keep it burning, and used its heat to continue to boil up batches of fresh sour mash. Take for
example the ever-feisty Jack Daniel's. Prohibition came to
Tennessee a solid decade before the rest of the country,

but rather than buckle and submit, the company simply skipped town and moved the distillery to St. Louis. When the law finally caught up with them there, they teamed up with none other than George Remus and his Kentucky Drug Company, who helped them to circumvent the government lockdown on their warehouses via a secret network of hoses and pipes that emptied right into waiting tanker trucks; the government inspectors were slow to catch on because the empty barrels had been filled with booze-scented water as a clever form of decoy. Pulling off the massive caper involved an unprecedented amount of bribery, causing Remus to later remark, "A few men have tried to corner the wheat market, only to find there is too much wheat in the world. I tried to corner the graft market, but learned there isn't enough money in the world to buy up all the officials who demand a share." And do you remember Old Crow? The brand continued to make fine Kentucky bourbon, although not in Kentucky; the American Medicinal Spirits Company opened an outpost in Canada and recruited Guy Beam, one of the Beam family's best distillers, to make it there. Once aged and tasted for quality, the Old Crow could be smuggled right back in across the border and sold to Americans, just as it had been for nearly a century.

While the big distillers may have done the best they could to keep the whiskey flowing, they were not the only ones pulling their weight in the bourbon department during the dry years of the '20s and early '30s. One of the many unintended side effects Prohibition had was to breathe new life into the long-standing American tradition of homemade spirits. In some cases, this took the form of small-scale bourbon production for personal use, as whimsically recalled by the great Southern writer Walker Percy:

Above: "The largest still ever taken in the national capital."
Below: During Prohibition, moonshining became a cottage industry nationwide, with small-time bootleggers jerry-rigging all manner of homemade stills for the production of whiskey.

Whiskey may have been illegal, but it was hardly
unavailable—this cache of illicit alcohol gives some idea
of the variety of brands a speakeasy might have on hand.

*1926: As a child, watching my father in Birmingham,
in the exurbs, living next to number-6 fairway of the
New Country Club, him disdaining both the bathtub
gin and white lightning of the time, aging his own
Bourbon in a charcoal keg, on his hands and knees
in the basement sucking on a siphon, a matter of
gravity requiring cheek pressed against cement floor,
the siphon getting going, the decanter ready, the first
hot spurt into his mouth not spat out.*

Not only was the demand for whiskey so great as to
make distillers out of suburban dads, it also invigorated
large-scale commercial moonshining in a way not seen
since the days of the Whiskey Rebellion. Across the South,
whole new still technologies were jerry-rigged and implemented to accommodate the realities and necessities of
Prohibition, including the Double-Stacked Mash Barrel

Still in Georgia, the Barrel-Capped Box Still in Virginia, and a version popular in North Carolina that used propane instead of wood to eliminate the telltale smoke that so often alerted government agents.* And in northern cities like Chicago, moonshining moved from backwoods hollows to ethnic tenements, where criminal entrepreneurs like the Genna brothers recruited entire families of Sicilian immigrants to make homemade whiskey. It was no great chore to convince southern Italians, long experienced in the arts of grappa making, to switch their recipes from Old World brandy to New World whiskey—especially given the fact that each bottle they produced could sell for as much as $60. Not a bad profit for bourbon that was more often grain alcohol mixed with creosote and caramel than it was the sincere attempt at true Kentucky sour mash that Percy the Elder did his best to turn out in his Southern basement.

The enforcement of the Volstead Act drastically altered the manner in which bourbon was produced and distributed, but it had an even greater effect on the way it was consumed. The drinking culture experienced a tremendous transformation during Prohibition, with the final result bearing far more resemblance to a contemporary bar scene than to the bare-knuckled brouhaha that existed only a few years before. The banishment of the diurnal and generally all-male saloon marked the arrival of the nocturnal and decidedly coed speakeasy, a place where men and women

---

* Smoke wasn't the only thing that gave away moonshiners—the process of making whiskey also turns the bark of nearby trees black, something Prohibition agents knew to look out for. Visit distilleries in Kentucky today, and one can't help but notice the miniature Black Forest that surrounds each and every one.

both could engage in clandestine canoodling by candle-light.* The mugs of beer with straight-up chasers favored in the old sawdust joints gave way to the barkeep's expertly mixed cocktail, a libation that disguised quite artfully the unpleasant taste of bootleg liquor. Quinine water, known as "tonic" back in colonial India when it was used to combat malaria, became a convenient way to hide the foul flavor of low-grade gin. Soft drinks, previously nothing more than a source of puerile diversion, quickly turned into a substitute for soda water, as their sweetness could readily mask a poorly made whiskey. Babe Ruth, the iconic baseball hero of the 1920s, allegedly started each morning with a whopping mug of ginger ale mixed with bourbon, a commanding drink to complement his sizable appetites. And in the 1930 film *Anna Christie*, Greta Garbo famously demands "a *viskey*, ginger ale on the side, and don't be stingy, baby," proof of just how ubiquitous such combos had become by the Roaring Twenties' close.

The very act of entering a drinking establishment also changed, graduating from a simple twist of the doorknob to a complex charade of exclusivity, complete with burly doormen capable of turning away those deemed suspicious or unworthy. Suddenly, to dance and drink meant entering a "club." The Stork Club, the 21 Club, the Country Club, the Bath Club—the names alone hint at an aura of selectivity and privilege. One observer described a New York speakeasy on East 53rd Street as "all marble and gold . . . Hat boys who

---

* One notable exception is McSorley's Old Ale House in New York City, which exercised a "men only" policy until 1970. The saloon's single-sex longevity is likely due to the fact that it never really had to become a speakeasy—during Prohibition, it was the favored watering hole for many of the city's Irish-American policemen and politicians, and continued to serve its famous ale with impunity.

won't touch a coat, and coat boys beneath whose station it is to handle a Borsalino." In clubs of this sort, elaborate security systems and admission protocols were established to protect against unwelcome visitors; the 21 Club even utilized an electronic alarm system capable of dumping the entire incriminating contents of its bar into a hidden series of basement grates at the mere push of a button. And instead of simply ordering a drink by its type—a whiskey, or a beer, or a gin—club-goers began requesting alcohol by label. This was a means of protecting oneself from poorly made hooch, but it was also a way to use alcohol as a status symbol, with the fancy—and smuggled—imported labels often commanding a greater price. Many club owners and bartenders were happy to take advantage of this new breed of drinking snobbery; when customers demanded bottle service, they made the sly use of labels "soaked in sea water to give an overseas appearance." Sound anything like a pretentious nightclub you've visited? It should. Because so much of the nightlife ritual we take for granted today can trace its origin to the dim, dusky realm that the prohibition against alcohol brought into being.

The first cultural whiffs of something new, modern, and profoundly American may have begun in the Prohibition-era barroom, but it didn't end at the door. The spirit of exuberance and creativity that illicit bourbon helped engender would spill past the twirling flappers and gruff bouncers, and make an indelible mark on the popular culture of the day. The stale, lily-white traditions that Prohibition's nativist advocates expounded were quickly drowned out by the very music that would lend the age its most defining sound: jazz. The first wave of the Great Migration following World War I brought thousands of disenfranchised Southern blacks to Northern cit-

Ladies' Night: Far from discouraging people from drinking, Prohibition liberated Jazz Age women to drink alongside men at coed speakeasies.

ies, fleeing from the grinding poverty and virulent racism of their rural homelands. When these hopeful migrants packed their trunks and purchased their train tickets, they brought the wailing beauty of New Orleans jazz and the aching cords of Delta blues with them, not to mention a taste for the house wine of the South, bourbon whiskey. Describing the most famous jazz venue of them all, Harlem's legendary Cotton Club, Duke Ellington would remember the following:

> *During the prohibition period, you could always*
> *buy good whiskey from somebody in the Cotton*
> *Club. They used to have what they called Chicken*
> *Cock. It was in a bottle in a can, and the can was*
> *sealed. It cost something like ten to fourteen dollars*
> *a pint. That was when I used to drink whiskey*
> *as though it were water. It seemed so weak to me*
> *after the twenty-one-year-old corn we had been*
> *accustomed to drinking down in Virginia. That was*
> *strong enough to move a train. . . .*

The bootleg whiskey of the jazz scene may not have held a candle to the aged bourbon Duke Ellington had been raised on, but it put the flame in his music, as it did for so many musicians of that era. Duke's own son, Mercer Ellington, a gifted jazz musician in his own right, would go on to become a representative for the bourbon brand J. W. Dant years later, following in his old man's footsteps as a lover of finely aged "corn." The arrival of that first cohort of Southern migrants would set the stage for the urban migrations of the Dust Bowl Oklahomans and factory-bound Appalachians that followed behind them. When the phonograph and the radio caught up to their genius, American popular music as we know it came into being, with predilections for bourbon both inspiring and disquieting its brightest stars in equal measure.*

Music wasn't the only American art form experiencing a renaissance; literature, too, was beginning to blossom, under the potent pens and prodigious thirsts of the Lost Generation.

---

* In the case of blues legend Robert Johnson, women and whiskey would prove his downfall in the most literal sense of the term—according to most accounts, he died shortly after drinking from a poisoned whiskey bottle offered to him by a jealous husband.

The First World War had left them disenfranchised in their own right, the character of their alienation far more spiritual than financial. And when it came to finding their way, bourbon whiskey provided them with a guiding light all its own, or at the very least, eased the suffering of their passage. Ernest Hemingway, who along with Gertrude Stein coined the name of his lost literary chums, was as keen on whiskey as his fictional counterparts, and famous for drinking it with water, soda, and at least once with lemonade—F. Scott Fitzgerald got the chills during a road trip, and Ernest thought it might serve as a restorative agent. And if stories are to be believed, when an editor once asked Hemingway how long it would take to finish a paragraph, he pointed to the whiskey bottle on his desk and answered, "About an inch or two."

As for F. Scott, despite his reputation as a high-class gin hound, his problematic drinking first manifested itself in 1918, at Louisville's Seelbach Hotel.* The bellboys could be counted on to smuggle bourbon bottles into officers' rooms, a scheme that resulted in his forced expulsion following one especially raucous bender. Fitzgerald would continue to drink bourbon throughout Prohibition, although he would confess in a short *New Yorker* piece from 1929 his disappointment with the "cases of dim, cut, unsatisfactory whisky" that the bootleggers sold.

John Dos Passos was also an aficionado of fine bourbon, and just "a small amount of magnificent Bourbon whisky" was enough to enliven his honeymoon and topple his writer's block. His buddy Ernest Hemingway once nearly got them both killed from drinking bourbon behind the wheel during a Montana road trip—the two writers had been taking nips to

---

* The luxurious Seelbach Hotel would also sneak its way into *The Great Gatsby*, inspiring the location of Tom and Daisy's Louisville wedding. No, George Remus was not invited.

ward off the November chill when Hemingway lost control and flipped the car. The crash resulted in a fractured arm for the intoxicated driver, but Dos Passos didn't even break his glasses—he claimed, quite absurdly, that the accident would have been worse had Hemingway not been relaxed and alert from the whiskey.

And when it comes to the king of all bourbon-loving writers, you can't beat the unabashedly Southern and indomitably parched William Faulkner. The ol' boy liked to go on week-long blackout benders, buying whiskey by the case to keep up with his thirst and burying the surplus in his garden for safe-keeping (an apparently ineffective measure, as a mischievous servant dug up his stash and drank it on at least one occasion). Faulkner once even drew a bank draft in the amount of $200 from his publisher to cover an overdue whiskey bill; evidently, the money that was supposed to go toward his bourbon habit had been lost while gambling. When his drinking problem became especially severe, he hired a nurse to follow him around town and administer smaller, more acceptable doses of whiskey from a black medical bag—a course of treatment that failed for obvious reasons. During his more manageable and dignified drunks, he was fond of sipping mint juleps, although straight sour mash would do just fine. "There is no such thing as bad whiskey," he once claimed; "some whiskeys just happen to be better than others." Luckily for American fiction, Faulkner's taste in prose proved far more discriminating than his taste in booze.

THE ONSET OF Prohibition was greeted by its supporters as the beginning of a more healthful and productive era in America. And for the first couple years or so, they may have had a point. When initial wartime measures were enacted against distilling in 1917, the death rate from alcoholism dropped from 5.2 deaths per 100,000 to 2.7. In 1920, when the ban against alcohol came into full effect, that number dropped ever further, to 1 death per 100,000. Productivity of the American workforce also took a leap in the right direction, with one industrialist testifying before the Prohibition commissioner that "before the Volstead Act, we had 10% absenteeism after pay day. Now it is not over 3%." Fewer hangovers meant fewer sick days, and even Henry Ford would weigh in, claiming somewhat hyperbolically, "I would not be able to build a car that will run 200,000 miles if booze were around, because I wouldn't have accurate workmen." The peculiar alliance of evangelists, industrialists, suffragettes, and nativists who had ushered in Prohibition gloated over the seeming success of their "noble experiment."

This collective pat on the back would prove to be horrifyingly premature, however. The salad days of early Prohibition did not last much longer than it took to whip up a batch of tainted hooch, beat down its competitors at the speakeasy next door, and bribe a cop to look the other way upon selling it. In short, even the most well-intentioned of experiments can have unforeseen results if not properly planned and executed, and the logic behind Prohibition was flawed from the start.

Where to begin? How about with the staggering toll in human life taken by poisonous batches of poorly made liquor. Federal law mandated that all alcohol made for industrial purposes be "denatured," and therefore toxic to consume, but that didn't stop bootleggers from using it and citizens from drinking it. On New Year's Day in 1927, 41 deaths were recorded in New York City at one hospital alone due to alcohol poisoning; the year whose close they were celebrating could claim 750 such deaths of its own, just in the Big Apple. And according to a 1928 Prohibition Bureau report, of the 480,000 gallons of illegal alcohol confiscated in New York City, 98 percent contained poisons. When the *New York World-Telegram* conducted a journalistic study of the problem, they found that of the some five hundred speak-easy samples they analyzed, fifty-five contained highly toxic wood alcohol in quantities sufficient to cause serious harm. It didn't take much analysis to see that the formerly regulated alcohol industry had been replaced by something far more nefarious; that initial dip in alcohol-related deaths, much vaunted by the Anti-Saloon League and its minions, would shoot right back up again once the bootleggers got in on the game. By the end of that tempestuous year of 1927, some estimate, no fewer than ten thousand and possibly as many as fifty thousand Americans had died from drinking poisonous bootleg alcohol, with many more suffering from blindness or paralysis as the result of a noble experiment that had gone horribly awry.

And then of course there was the most damning of Prohibition's many flaws—it simply did not work. The American people, though momentarily hobbled in their saloon habits, did not stop drinking—not by a long shot. Not in cities, not in towns, not in the country. In Boise, Idaho, a police chief complained that "drinking is done almost everywhere, by almost everybody." Several states away in Topeka, Kansas, another police chief lamented that "the girls simply won't go out with the boys who haven't got flasks to offer." And in the big cities back east, bars seemed to increase in number when they should have vanished altogether. Prior to the implementation of the Volstead Act, New York City could claim some fifteen thousand legal drinking establishments. In 1922, after the introduction of Prohibition, the city served as home to roughly five thousand speakeasies. By 1927, however, that number had jumped to at least thirty thousand—twice the number of bars as when alcohol was legal. It's impossible to know exactly how many illicit liquor joints filled New York's alleys during its speakeasy heyday, but there are estimates that set it as high as one hundred thousand. The Anti-Saloon League did indeed put the bustling saloons, festive beer gardens, and lively taverns temporarily out of business. In doing so, however, it unwittingly gave birth to a boozy Hydra beyond comprehension and containment, a beast made possible by the almost inconceivable amount of wealth that the illegal alcohol trade generated.

The government-regulated liquor industry was replaced by a ruthless new class of mega-gangsters, the likes of which had never before been encountered by American law enforcement. Men like Al Capone and Bugs Moran were able to keep their operations running smoothly because of the insurmountable sums they had at their disposal. A Prohibition agent could make as much as $300,000 a month in bribes, and more than a few did. As records would later show, between 1920 and 1930, some 11,926 agents—out of a force of 17,816—were "separated without prejudice" because of suspected criminal involvement, and another 1,587 were "dismissed for cause" when their criminal involvement was too blatant to sweep under the rug. Even churches got in on the action, many using their sacramental wine permits as a license to bamboozle—the archbishop of San Francisco himself instructed all of the priests in his diocese to buy their Communion wine from his vintner pal Georges de Latour, in quantities far exceeding what was needed for Sunday Mass. When it was revealed that the president of the United States, Warren G. Harding, had kept a private stash of fine bourbon hidden in the White House during Prohibition, few were surprised . . . and many were no doubt jealous. In an age when America supposedly went dry, the nation's wettest citizens were guiding its course.

Toxicity, duplicity, disruption, corruption—the failed experiment of Prohibition was tearing at the seams of social order, criminalizing priests, doctors, police, and your bourbon-loving great-grandfather, to say nothing of fueling the most violent gangster underworld the country had seen. And yet the national ban on alcohol kept chugging along, while the rest of Western civilization looked on in head-shaking confusion. What would it take to bring those Yanks to their senses?

Unfortunately, it would take a disaster: the Great Depression. On October 29, 1929—also known as Black Tuesday—the stock market crashed in unprecedented fashion, and sent the U.S. economy into a dizzying free fall. The speculative boom of the Roaring Twenties turned virtually overnight into a staggering catastrophe. Jobs were lost, fortunes squandered, lives ruined . . . and as the same geniuses in government who had championed Prohibition scratched their heads and attempted to make sense of the matter, a glaring fact emerged from the ashes of the American economy: Prior to the Volstead Act, the beverage alcohol industry, bourbon in particular, had put a tremendous amount of treasure into the U.S. Treasury. Prohibition had negated that contribution, causing the federal government to miss out on roughly half a billion dollars a year in revenue. Throw in the cost of all the extra (and largely ineffectual) law enforcement needed to secure the ban, figure in the lost revenue on the smuggled liquor that replaced all that formerly taxable domestic alcohol, and you're talking about a net loss during Prohibition estimated to be over *$11 billion*. And that, as our democratically elected brain trust in Washington was beginning to see, was hardly chicken feed.

FROM THE MOMENT our nation secured its independence, the American whiskey industry had been called on to fork over a bit extra during times of need. The taxes that sparked

Pouring money down the drain: Unable to tax alcohol, the government lost out on billions of dollars during Prohibition. When the Great Depression hit and federal revenues dried up, booze was seen as a savior, and the repeal of the Eighteenth Amendment wasn't far behind. The renewed flow of tax dollars from bourbon and other spirits helped fund relief programs and public-works projects.

the Whiskey Rebellion were intended to pay back the debt left over from our own war with England; the heavy excises levied in the aftermath of the Civil War helped to pay for the South's reconstruction. And with America's economy suddenly reeling, the whiskey industry would be called on again to come to its assistance. The income tax first collected in 1913 worked only so long as citizens actually had income. With very little of that to be had, President Franklin Roosevelt did what needed to be done, and what many had been silently wishing for for more than a decade. The Eighteenth Amendment was repealed on December 5, 1933, to far less celebration than one might expect. Instead, it was met with weary relief, nauseated regret, and a sense that the nation had gone horribly astray. A letter from John D. Rockefeller, a fellow with some serious skin in the game when it came to the economy, says it all:

> When Prohibition was introduced, I hoped that it would be widely supported by public opinion and that the day would soon come when the evil effects of alcohol would be recognized. I have slowly and reluctantly come to believe that this has not been the result. Instead, drinking has generally increased; the speakeasy has replaced the saloon; a vast army of lawbreakers has appeared; many of our best citizens have openly ignored Prohibition; respect for the law has been greatly lessened; and crime has increased to a level never seen before.

Many of Prohibition's most vocal advocates were forced to admit not just to defeat, but to the fact that the ban on alcohol had achieved the exact opposite of that for which it was intended. That was the great irony of their failed social experiment—instead of decreasing crime, it only made crime bigger and more organized; instead of empowering women financially as homemakers, it only emboldened them to bob their hair and drink alongside the men. And far from curtailing the aspirations of America's Catholic and Jewish immigrants, it would eventually help to put a Kennedy in the White House[*] and Las Vegas on the map. The America that emerged from it looked far more like the vibrant and diverse nation we know today, and virtually nothing like the quaint Sunday school class that its strange coalition of backers had envisioned.

No, no, no, Prohibition had been a mistake, a grave miscalculation, and with its repeal, America was ready for its

---

[*] Didn't know JFK's old man was a bootlegger? There was a lot of money to be made in "medicinal" scotch, and those Harvard tuition bills weren't cheap.

beloved bourbon to come flowing forth. But there was one small problem: properly aged, bourbon takes a heck of a long time to make, and after fourteen-plus years of still smashing and barrel axing, there was very little bourbon left to sell, and few distilleries standing with the resources to produce more of it. A realization upon which congressmen, senators, and acting presidents must have all smacked their own foreheads and quite audibly groaned, having grasped the great damage they had done to the American Spirit.

Even with Prohibition's repeal in 1933, the prognosis remained bleak for the country's crippled economy and whiskey industry alike. The worst days of the Great Depression saw our national unemployment rate reach 25 percent, stock prices fall by 85 percent, and the failure of a quarter of all banks. Meanwhile, in the bourbon heartland of Kentucky, of the seventeen major distilleries that had been producing whiskey prior to Prohibition, only seven were functioning by 1935. The once flourishing city of Louisville, where F. Scott Fitzgerald had learned to savor the flavor of barrel-aged sour mash, was rendered abject by bourbon's near collapse—eight thousand jobs were lost in that city alone when the distillers shut their doors, an industrial disaster that would claim 5 percent of the jobs in the state. With most of the extant aged whiskey from the government-controlled bond houses already long-since liquidated to medicinal alcohol companies, and the resources to begin distilling new bourbon simply nonexistent, a novel approach was needed—something innovative and drastic had to be done. From the chaos of the '20s and the penury of the '30s, a truth about bourbon, and America, became self-evident: For both to survive in the twentieth century, a more inclusive vision for the future would be demanded. Americans of disparate backgrounds and beliefs would have to set aside their differences, and work together for the common good.

While President Franklin Delano Roosevelt buddied up to unions and social reformers as part of his New Deal, the traditional distilling families of bourbon country decided to forge some unlikely alliances of their own. They had the experience, the heritage, and the desire to begin producing barrel-aged bourbon once again; what they lacked was the investment capital to get their distilleries up and running—after more than a decade out of business, they simply had no money. In the industrial cities just to their north, however, there were successful businessmen from recent immigrant backgrounds who did possess the much-needed funds, as well as the necessary appreciation for the spirit's potential. Their arrival on the American scene had not been via wagon train through the Cumberland Gap; it was via Ellis Island, through the close-knit ethnic communities that Prohibition's xenophobic progenitors had so deeply despised. And instead of titles like Beam, Crow, Taylor, and Brown, they went by names like Shapira,* Getz, Abelson, and Wertheimer. New and lasting business relationships took root between the bourbon patriarchs and their unlikely saviors, as best epitomized by the famous Jim Beam. At the spry young age of seventy, he along with his direct kin partnered with the Chicago investors Phillip Blum, Oliver Jacobson, and Harry Homel to resurrect the whiskey brand that he considered his birthright. On August 14, 1934, the James B. Beam Distilling Company was incorporated; in a mind-blowingly short period of just 120 days, a new distilling facility was erected. And in early March 1935, the mashing of what was soon to

---

* Just how meaningful and long-lasting many of these partnerships became can be seen at the Heaven Hill Distillery—descendants of the original Shapira brothers who invested in the company would continue to own and run it into the twenty-first century. And guess who was manning those stills? Members of the same Beam family who were running them back in 1935.

become bourbon once again commenced. Similar stories would be repeated across Kentucky's bourbon landscape, with many of the spirit's most legendary brands partnering with larger corporations to begin producing whiskey once again. True, it did consolidate the state's whiskey output into a mere handful of corporate-owned distilleries, and yes, it did have an effect on quality. But it also kept bourbon alive, after having been brought to the brink of total and irreparable ruin. The spirit survived, due in part to the resilience and tenacity that had become our nation's hallmark, but, more important, by dint of a truly modern vision for all that "American" could mean. The country needed a bridge between the "Old" America and the "New," and as it just so happened, during that first and most tenuous half of the twentieth century, bourbon would come to span that cultural divide quite perfectly, joining two worlds in a common identity.

So what's next for bourbon? Where do we go from here? What could possibly trump the chaotic clamor of the Roaring Twenties, or the Great Depression's grinding despair?

How about the biggest war the world has ever known, a bomb big enough to seal our own doom, a consumer culture that only seems to be growing, and an entire generation that's about to go . . .

BOOM!

8

G.I. Joe Gets His First DUI

THE HAWAIIAN ISLANDS greeted the Sunday morning
of December 7, 1941, much as they had for millen-
nia: with cool winds, languid sunshine, and the mile-off
murmur of soft-breaking waves. Only, on that particular
morning, a drone whispered from the blue of the horizon.
At first, the American servicemen on duty—more than a
few of whom were still hungover from a Saturday night of
whiskey and beer in the bars of Honolulu—paid it little
heed. Such sounds were commonplace around the naval
base of Pearl Harbor, and given the volatile state of European and Asian affairs, early-morning training missions
were not uncommon. But something about its insistence,
and mounting intensity, stoked their concern. They
paused briefly from their quotidian duties of hoisting
flags and polishing gun barrels, and took a squinting
appraisal of the bass-humming sky. As to the source of
the hum, it revealed itself shortly, amid a torrent of burnt
lead and a deluge of fire.

The first wave of Japanese torpedo bombers came across

the island just before eight in the morning. Their silverfish payloads slipped gracefully into the water, only to violently gouge out entire hulls of battleships and destroyers. The chugging grunts of antiaircraft guns could scarcely catch the tail end of their dives. Minutes later, the second wave of attack planes stormed down, their machine guns strafing U.S. military bases and setting grounded aircraft aflame. For ninety minutes the unrelenting barrage continued, turning the seas to a welter of flaming oil, and the palm-frayed shoreline, previously so peaceful, into a scorched Golgotha.

Half an ocean away, aboard the American troopship *Republic*, part of the Pensacola convoy, wireless communications were abruptly interrupted by a message whose urgency cut blade-like through the static: *"Japan started hostilities . . . govern yourself accordingly."* In the saloon compartment, where an early-morning church service had only just begun, two colonels interrupted to break the news. In a dash the sailors and servicemen returned to their stations, initiating their well-rehearsed steps to prepare the ship for battle. Within minutes, all flammable wooden deck timbers were ripped up and heaved overboard; ropes spiraled downward from the deck, followed by shirtless men with buckets of camouflage gray paint. Machine guns were broken out from the hold and remounted on the bow, gleaming and lethal in the morning sunlight. Upon prying apart the crates of ammunition, however, a surprising although hardly unwelcome discovery was made—some resourceful and forward-thinking sailor had stashed two crates of prime Kentucky bourbon among the polished brass cartridges and layers of packed straw.

For an awkward moment the men gazed mutely down at the whiskey. They were on the cusp of joining the greatest war the world had witnessed, one that would keep them from their homes for years, rent apart the lives of millions, and wreak havoc on virtually every corner of the globe. Someone ought

V-J Day, August 1945: Servicemen celebrate by "liberating"
whiskey from a San Francisco liquor store.

to at least drink the damn stuff before it all went to hell. The
whiskey was opened, passed around in a sort of patriotic communion, and the entire machine-gun crew was treated to "a
spiritual uplifting they hadn't expected," as one of the brave
souls among them would later recall.

In the aftermath of the attack on Pearl Harbor and the

declaration of war against the Axis powers, many others would follow the crew of the *Republic*'s lead, temporarily putting their peacetime lives on hiatus to assist more meaningfully in the war effort. Schoolteachers would become paratroopers; plumbing manufacturers would transform into munitions factories; rosy-cheeked homemakers would reinvent themselves convincingly as Rosie the Riveters. And bourbon, forever crucial in wartime, would do its part as well, setting beverage whiskey aside to contribute directly toward victory. And peace, once won, would usher in an era of unprecedented prosperity and global influence. The American Spirit, hobbled by decades of prohibition and depression, would finally reach its full potential, as all those thirsty G.I.s came home, got hitched, bought houses in the suburbs, and two or three highballs into it, started doing a whole lot of baby making.

What age is this, so chock-full o' automobiles, sitcoms, and the mass-marketed sheen of Madison Avenue? Sure, it is an atomic one, with a world ideologically cloven and antsy about the bomb, but also a golden one—a golden age for consumerism and bourbon both. When not keeping up with the Soviets, we were keeping up with the Joneses, and as it just so happened, the Joneses liked their station wagons to be from Detroit, their news courtesy of Cronkite, their neighborhoods unconditionally suburban, and their liquor cabinets stocked with straight Kentucky bourbon.

WHEN ONE THINKS of alcohol, the image most commonly conjured is one of bar scenes, booze bottles, and Breathalyzers. Seldom are its industrial applications considered, and yet they are many, and indeed as crucial to military operations in the mid-twentieth century as they are today. How so? Well, before we sling our carbines over our shoulders, light up a Lucky Strike, and head off to war, it might prove useful to consider a few figures . . . and carefully at that, because this stuff is as flammable as all get-out. Need a vehicle to get that corncob-chomping five-star general to the front? You're going to require a good-sized drum of grain neutral spirit, because 23 gallons of industrial alcohol go into making just one Jeep. Plan on softening up those fortifications on Guadalcanal before your boys go in. For each and every 16-inch naval shell that comes off the line, 19¾ gallons are required. And if you're keen on getting those Krauts out of their bunker before you storm the beaches of Normandy, you'll be using 1 gallon of grain neutral spirit for every two 155mm howitzer shells you fire off, and every sixty-four hand grenades you lob Nazi-ward. Rubber for tires, rayon for parachutes, fuel for aircraft, and of course all that antifreeze to keep tanks running in the Battle of the Bulge—all equally dependent on industrial alcohol, and all obligatory for winning such a truly global struggle. Booze had come a long way since the days of the Civil War, and it could do a whole lot more than anesthetize casualties and intoxicate generals, although it would continue to do a fair amount of both. Alcohol was to become a crucial component in winning the war against the Axis powers, and lucky for America, there was one industry with the resources, equipment, and experience to make it. Nope, not the automotive industry, not the steel industry, and certainly not the hospitality industry, but the bourbon industry—it would be the one to come to the rescue and get down in the trenches, churning out high-proof ethanol in unprecedented quantities. The U.S. government issued the mandate, and America's distillers answered the call,* putting all whiskey making aside to devote themselves solely to the manufacture of industrial alcohol for the war effort.

---

* Bourbon wasn't the only Kentucky-based industry to pitch in—Louisville Slugger put its bat making on temporary hiatus to turn out rifle stocks instead.

A whiskey distillery enlisted to produce industrial alcohol for the cause.

Over the course of WWII, American distillers would contribute 650 million gallons of alcohol for synthetic rubber, 126 million gallons for antifreeze, 102 million gallons for explosives, 75 million gallons for plastics, 70 million gallons for textiles, 66 million gallons for fuel, and an additional 115 million gallons for the assorted chemicals that kept the American war machine in motion. The larger distilleries were able to adapt their perpetual stills quite easily to produce industrial alcohol rather than whiskey; the smaller distilleries created the highest-proof alcohol they could, and then shipped it to the bigger distilleries for further processing. This massive conversion from beverage to industrial alcohol production was initiated by legislative mandates, but they were hardly necessary; American whiskey makers were happy to do their part in what they considered to be a patriotic duty, as evinced by a PSA from a 1943 edition of *Life* magazine. In addition to a checklist of ways common citizens could assist in the war effort—things like planting Victory

gardens and buying war bonds—it also includes the following message on behalf of the National Distillers Products
Corporation, and a symbolic G.I. by the name of Bill:

> *Bill never did like big talk. Fourth of July orators
> made him squirm. Election-day speakers made him
> mad. He hated big words and fancy talk. Nobody
> had to sell the war to Bill. He saw his duty and left
> a good paying job to go and do it. If you were to
> ask Bill today to set down in writing the things he is
> fighting for, he probably wouldn't talk about great
> concepts like the Four Freedoms, or free enterprise,
> or the dignity of man. He'd say simply: "I am
> fighting for my home and my wife and the kids I
> hope we'll have some day. I am fighting for my right
> to sit in a sunlit picnic grove with my family . . . my
> right to criticize, over a coke or a highball, the
> Brooklyn Dodgers or the men in Washington . . . the
> privilege of watching my son grow in the image of
> me and my wife instead of some dictator." These are
> a few of the thousands of "little freedoms" that add
> up to the American way of life—and that essentially
> is what Bill is fighting for. He'll do his job and we
> folks back home must get on with our job. . . .
> We at National Distillers don't like big talk any
> more than Bill does. We wish to state simply that
> we, like the rest of the distilling industry, are
> devoting our entire production facilities 100%
> to war alcohol—used for munitions, rubber,
> medicines and many other essential war needs,
> and are producing no whiskey today.*

A stoic tribute indeed, and printed beneath it, a list of the
familiar bottled-in-bond bourbon brands that the National

Distillers Products Corporation proudly represents—Old Grand-Dad, Old Taylor, and Old Crow—with the caveat that all whiskey stock for sale was distilled before the attack on Pearl Harbor.

The sacrifices of the wartime generation were monumental, and the violence took a tremendous toll—more than four hundred thousand Americans lost their lives for the cause. The tax levied upon the nation in blood and treasure was heavy, but island by island in the Pacific, town by town in Europe, the American war machine proved itself unequaled. Victory in Europe was secured on May 8, 1945; the Japanese surrendered on August 15. The war was over, and the industrial alcohol of the wartime bourbon industry had helped produce the shells that were fired, the bombs that were dropped, the parachutes that were deployed, and the tires that were needed in the effort. From the riveters who made it to the G.I.s who used it, much of the wartime equipment deployed contained a healthy splash of the American Spirit.

THE SECOND WORLD WAR may have been won, but soon two former allies, the triumphant Americans and Soviets, were squaring off. While the world was being carved up along ideological lines so, too, were the global drinking tastes divided between good old bourbon whiskey and Comrade Vodka. Forever full of bravado, General George Patton gave an account of a drinking contest with the Russians following the defeat of the Axis powers playfully portending the tensions that lay ahead:

> *After the ceremony . . . we went to the officer's*
> *club . . . and had lunch, which consisted mostly*
> *of whiskey. The Russians tried to drink American*
> *whiskey without water with very bad results. I*

unquestionably drank the Russian commander
under the table and walked out under my own
steam. We are going to pay back a call on the
14th, prior to which date I will drink quite a lot of
mineral oil, as they will unquestionably try to get
us drunk.

And from a letter that followed:

Every one wanted me to get vodka for them to drink
but I decided they could drink whiskey or nothing.
The results were great. The [Russian] general went
out cold and I . . . did not even have a head ake [sic].
I kept putting water in my bourbon and he did not.

Certainly a chuckle-inducing anecdote, though it belies the gravity of the new world order that came into being in the postwar years. On the one side of that bristling dividing line, there were the Soviets, with their interminable food lines, impossibly drab architecture, sprawling labor camps, and gallons of colorless low-grade vodka. On the other side, there was free speech, democratic elections, and open markets that spread amber bourbon and other products of American culture across the Free World. American power was not just symbolic, however: a network of military bases spread across the map—West Germany, Italy, Japan, South Korea, the Middle East, and elsewhere. And wherever servicemen were stationed, bourbon soon followed by the case. As was the case for so many distinctly American consumer products, that good ol' aged corn liquor from back home was beginning to pick up an international following.

The new American presence abroad may have given bourbon a boost, but it paled in comparison to what all those thirsty G.I.s would do for it once they hung up their rifles and returned to the home front. Having lived through

KENTUCKY QUALITY IS TOP OF THE WORLD

WORLD'S LARGEST SELLING KENTUCKY WHISKEY

OLD
Sunny Brook
BRAND

"Cheerful as its Name"

THE OLD SUNNY BROOK COMPANY, LOUISVILLE, KENTUCKY

"Top of the world": After World War II, bourbon emerged as a global booze superpower. America wasn't doing too badly, either.

the homespun and hardtack of the Great Depression, and the rifle shots and rationing of the greatest war of all, they'd earned the right to some mass-produced peace and quiet, and in suburbia, they found it in spades. Remember our friend Bill from the bourbon PSA, who dreamed of returning home to his wife, having a kid, and drinking highballs in a sunlit grove? That's exactly what he did. And with an economy thriving thanks to all that wartime stimulation, and a powerful consumer culture congealing around the "nuclear" family, Bill and bourbon are both about to raise a glass and shoot for the moon.

THE CONCEPT OF suburbia didn't begin in the postwar years—American suburbs had first appeared along commuter rail lines outside major cities in the late nineteenth century—but it was in the war's immediate aftermath that suburban living became the norm. Between 1940 and 1950, the suburban population in the United States increased by 35 percent. In the two decades that followed, that growth would continue unabated, with New York City's suburban population increasing by 4.26 million, that of Los Angeles by 4.2 million, and Chicago's by 1.77 million, to name a few. And what drew all these family men to settle in what the snarkier among us might deem such conformist and mundane surroundings? In short, it was a perfect combination of cheap mass-produced automobiles, affordable housing developments, and the relatively new federal policy of supporting home ownership. Perhaps that old pioneering lust for land to call one's own, no matter how small or rectangular the acreage, factored in as well, but either way, the decades of the '50s and '60s belonged to the burbs. In communities like Levittown, Long Island, during peak periods of construction, a new house was finished every fifteen minutes. Buying such a home cost a mere $7,990, and for former G.I.s, it could be mortgaged with no money down and a monthly payment of just $56. And with an average yearly salary in the mid-1950s close to $4,000, that left plenty of extra money to have two or three kids, purchase an American-made automobile, buy a gray flannel suit, and invest quite generously in the new culture of middle-class consumerism that was transforming what had been a nation of relatively poor farmers and even poorer immigrants into the sitcom-loving, fast-food-gobbling, pop-music-craving, and gas-guzzling country we are, in many ways, to this very day.

Gas-guzzling? Indeed. For when the ruthlessly efficient assembly lines of Detroit transformed the automobile from a plaything of the rich to a middle-income necessity, the physical and social landscape of the nation changed along with it. Neighborhoods widened, commutes lengthened, and everything became farther apart—including bars. The corner saloon was no longer a five-minute walk from the tenement apartment; it was a five-mile drive off a long cul-de-sac. And drinking and driving, well, even those of us who gently slumbered through driver's ed know that those two don't mix particularly well. So what did these hard-drinking and flannel-suited company men do instead? They boozed at home, and in doing so, created an entirely new American institution: the cocktail party. Incorporating simple two-ingredient cocktails known as "highballs," couples began entertaining in their dens and living rooms. They invited over a few neighbors, threw a record on the hi-fi, and did pretty much the same thing their parents had done in speakeasies, but in the shag-carpeted comfort of their own three-bedroom ranch-style houses. Drinking in America during the middle of the twentieth century took on an overtly domestic character, and the large corporations that owned the bourbon brands of Kentucky and Tennessee were well aware that the keys to suburban liquor cabinets were not sitting on any Formica countertop, but rather dangling from the glossy fingers of Madison Avenue's admen. Everyone and their grandfather knew what bourbon was. Convincing a conformist generation that everyone who mattered was drinking it, well, that was a different matter entirely.

ACCORDING TO AN article titled "The Effect of Advertising on Liquor Brand Sales" published in the *Journal of Marketing Research* (vol. 6, no. 3) in 1969, no study of the correlation between advertising dollars and whiskey-case sales can commence without first understanding this basic formula, with $S_{j,t}$ representing sales of brand j in year t:

$$S_{j,t} = f(S_{j,t-1}, A_{j,t}, R_{k,t}, P_{j,t}, F_{j,t}, \dots)$$

A little confused? Not to worry. Perhaps this ratio for estimating decay and retention rates in the whiskey market will make the turbid waters of advertising science a little less murky, with $R_{k,t}$ representing sales of product-type k in adjusted cases (thousands) in year t:

$$\frac{\frac{1}{10}\sum_{t=1}^{10} R_{k,t-1}}{R_{k,t-1}}$$

Still no joy? While these formulas are utterly inscrutable to the mathematically impaired (your Faithful Author included), they do give some indication of just how much whiskey marketing had changed since barrels were taken to market atop mule backs. As to how and when this transformation in bourbon advertising occurred, it was a gradual process that closely mirrored the concurrent shifts in American industry and consumer culture.

Traditional bourbon advertising was . . . traditional.

The first advertisements for bourbon came into being not long after bourbon itself, with public notices pitching the liquid fruits of the Old Bourbon region appearing in local newspapers in the early 1800s. Text-based, with limited visual imagery or persuasive language, such posts were strictly informative—glorified classified ads more than anything else, designed to alert the drinking public of the whiskey's availability for purchase. The first real advertisements in the modern sense of the word made their appearance toward the end of the nineteenth century, roughly around the time that Colonel Taylor and George Garvin Brown were giving their respective bourbon brands a personality and life of their own. For the first time the marketing message wasn't strictly to inform, but also to persuade; whiskey was no longer an interchangeable commodity, but a branded product with differentiated qualities. Advertising became bound by a new art of human persuasion: "Machine-made products, turned out by the millions, must be assimilated to the destiny of things not machinelike," wrote one adman in the early twentieth century; they "must be translated . . . into human terms." To accommodate this new emotional approach, advertisements featuring graphically designed artwork became the standard, more often than not capitalizing on bourbon's down-home heritage. Wholly nostalgic, they featured either bucolic depictions of frontier life, or rosy-eyed references to the bygone age of antebellum Kentucky gentlemen, both of which expressed in an intangible way what consumers of that period wanted out of their whiskey.

Imagery and messaging of the nostalgic sort sufficed for the first half of the twentieth century, but the social and cultural changes that swept America in the wake of the Second World War rendered such advertising antiquated, if not flat-out repugnant. The new emerging suburban middle class had little desire to see Appalachian log cabins or colonels admiring fine horses; both were contradictory to the spirit of progress that had gripped the era. Why romanticize the past when the future was so bright? What appealed to them were the aspirational trappings of modern, successful life—happy, attractive, and social couples, entertaining their equally enviable peers in their new houses, surrounded by futuristic gadgets. And when the major corporations that controlled virtually all the whiskey distilling in America—Seagram, Schenley, National, Hiram Walker, and Brown-Forman—teamed up with the ad whizzes on Madison Avenue to target said demographic, that

One for the road: Bourbon targets a
new consumer during the Automobile Age.

was precisely what the consumer got. The famous copywriting pioneer John Star Hewitt nailed it perfectly, observing that the average American consumer compensated "for the routine of today by the vision of what his life is to be tomorrow. It is the vision of getting ahead. Everything he buys comes as a partial fulfillment of that vision."

There was one problem, however: When it came time for Mr. Jet Age to open his liquor cabinet, he found the same booze his great-grandfather drank. Reinventing a traditional product like bourbon wasn't easy, for while America had relaxed considerably since the days of Carrie Nation, her hatchet had yet to dull entirely. Federal laws placed severe restrictions on when and where high-proof spirits could be advertised, particularly when it came to the incredibly effective realm of broadcast media. A disappointment no doubt for those chain-smoking and highball-slugging admen, but it wouldn't prove insurmountable. The new consumer emphasis on "lifestyle" had produced a rash of omnipresent lifestyle magazines. *Life*, *Look*, *Esquire*, and *Vogue* became permanent fixtures on end tables, while spicier titles like *Playboy* were found in the bottom of millions of desk drawers.

And what did they all have in common? Glossy sheen aside, each could claim a healthy portion of bourbon advertisements slickly and subtly appealing to the suburban tastes and consumer-based lifestyles of its loyal readership. Just how much the periodicals market expanded during the era can be seen in the following figures: In 1952, "straight and bonded whiskey advertising," in other words, bourbon, accounted for exactly $132,597 in magazine ad sales and $850,259 in newspaper ad sales. By 1961, less than a decade later, those numbers had leaped remarkably to $4,029,197 and $4,096,921, for magazines and newspapers respectively. Together, that's an eightfold increase in total print media ad buying, and a whole lot of consumers that, between loving Lucy and leaving it to Beaver, could absorb carefully crafted magazine ads featuring successful, attractive, and yes, invariably white suburbanites, only slightly more successful and attractive than themselves, enjoying tall glasses of bourbon in the most sanguine and socially acceptable environments.

An advert from the 1960s for Sunny Brook bourbon says it all: "People like *you*," it so confidently claims beneath a scene of well-dressed suburban couples laughing together, "like Sunny Brook!" The only log cabins and corncob pipes to be found in media were on *The Beverly Hillbillies*, where the stereotypical trappings of Appalachian frontier life served as a source of high comedy and pure derision for its freshly anointed middle-class viewers, many of whose parents and grandparents, quite ironically, had shared more in common with the Clampetts than they ever had with the Cleavers. As anyone on Madison Avenue can tell you, a little insecurity can go a long way, and in the '50s and '60s, with "ease" and "modernity" the orders of the day, Americans were far more interested in looking forward to a shimmering, fresh-from-the-factory future than casting embarrassed half-glances at our immigrant and rural past.

As for whether or not bourbon's new advertising strategy worked, well, the short answer is "it did," and the longer answer is "boy, did it ever." A list of the twenty leading liquor brands in the United States between 1960 and 1962 is full of straight and bonded bourbon labels, including such familiars as Old Crow, Jim Beam, Early Times, Ancient Age, Four Roses, Old Taylor, and Ten High. Not that there wasn't competition, however. Between the years of 1952 and 1961, bourbon's Cold War foe vodka gained considerably in popularity thanks to the suburban demand for female-friendly cocktails, increasing its output by 18.9 million gallons. As for scotch and Canadian whiskey, both of which had picked up a following during the smuggling years of Prohibition, they too saw a considerable bump in production, accounting for increases of 12.4 million and 5.3 million gallons, respectively. But when it came to bourbon whiskey, the American Spirit would blow them all out of the water, with output for straight and bonded whiskeys increasing by a staggering 37.5 million gallons. And with blended domestic whiskey, which had become commonplace in wartime due to bourbon shortages, falling precipitate from favor in the new postwar economy, bourbon had nowhere to go but up, capturing much of the market share from its cheaper rectified cousin. In 1945, straight and bonded bourbon could claim a mere 9.9 percent of the output share for bottled whiskey, with low-quality blended whiskey accounting for most of the rest. By 1950, bourbon's percentage had climbed considerably to reach

PEOPLE LIKE YOU LIKE SUNNY BROOK!

People with a taste for today's good living, people like you—like Sunny Brook. This flawless Kentucky whiskey has a nation-wide reputation for superb taste. Sunny Brook is so fine, it has a World's Fair Grand Prize to its credit. You can even buy the type of whiskey you prefer. Choose the mild, smooth straight bourbon or the extra mild blend. The prices are surprisingly reasonable. Yes, people like you like Sunny Brook. Try it.

THE OLD SUNNY BROOK DISTILLERY COMPANY, LOUISVILLE, KY. • KENTUCKY STRAIGHT BOURBON WHISKEY, 86 PROOF • KENTUCKY BLENDED WHISKEY 86 PROOF, 65% GRAIN NEUTRAL SPIRITS

How do you like your whiskey?
Smooth and mild?
BUY THE STRAIGHT

Smooth and extra mild?
BUY THE BLEND

Leave it to bourbon: Madison Avenue mastered
the art of appealing to suburban parents.

24.4 percent. And by 1961, straight and bonded bourbon whiskeys accounted for 49.8 percent of the total bottled whiskey output—virtually half.

The bourbon boom that began in the '50s would only become all the more resounding through the decade of the '60s, as the golden age of the American Spirit reached its full, global potential. In 1962, the same year President Kennedy won the atomic game of chicken known as the Cuban missile crisis, bourbon whiskey moved into first place in terms of national popularity, bumping scotch and Canadian whiskey off the map. In 1966, the year Cassius Clay knocked the stuffing out of the British boxer Henry Cooper, bourbon could claim a 239 percent increase in sales in less than two decades, growth that rendered the upticks of English gin and Russian vodka mere mole hills. And in 1969, the same year American Neil Armstrong executed his own rather clumsy version of the moonwalk, the Bourbon Institute released a report claiming that "over the last 10 year period, Bourbon sales enjoyed its greatest period of growth." Ever, mind you. And it was no longer being sipped solely by Americans. At the decade's close, bourbon whiskey was also being exported to 102 foreign nations. West Germany led the pack, thanks to the massive American military deployment there, but other countries were right on its heels. In just one year, bourbon consumption had increased in Australia by 54 percent, in Mexico by 42 percent, in the United Kingdom by 48 percent, and in New Zealand with a positively jaw-dropping surge of 334 percent. Even those notoriously fussy and epicurean French tipped their berets to the new bourbon dynasty, upping their intake by 22 percent. Thirsty nations such as these accounted for a sizable chunk of the 84.2 million gallons sold between 1969 and 1970, as bourbon whiskey, reaching an all-time peak, grew well beyond its native borders and established itself as a global presence.

How was bourbon able to so convincingly assert its identity worldwide? U.S. military might and the booming popularity of American culture certainly had something to do with it, although a little-known act passed by the United States Congress back in 1964 may have done just as much. After a testy and tumultuous two-century relationship, the boys in Washington finally got around to giving bourbon the credit it deserved, officially declaring it a "distinctive product of the United States." Just what did that mean? Basically, for bourbon to be sold as bourbon, be it at the corner liquor store in Anytown, USA, a mod new club on London's Carnaby Street, or the finest geisha house in Kyoto, it had to be made in America. Grant you, an ambitious young distiller anywhere on earth could whip up some corn-based sour mash, run it through a still, and let it sit in a new charred-oak barrel for a couple years. Heck, he could even bottle it, ship it, and put it up for sale. But unless it was 100 percent made in the USA according to the proper standards, he could not label it as "bourbon whiskey" in any corner of the globe where the United States and its multifarious trade agreements held sway. For the very first time perhaps since the spirit's inception, when someone in the Free World purchased a bottle of bourbon whiskey, he could be virtually certain that a very real piece of America was contained within.

AND SO, WITH bourbon back on top, and the United States in firm command both at home and abroad, let's close out the American Spirit's most ascendant era by taking a respite from the barrage of facts and figures. An anecdote, you say? Gladly. Let's head south.

In 1966, the state of Mississippi, full of pluck although hardly progressive, at last caught up with the rest of the country and lifted its Prohibition-era ban on alcoholic beverages. This was done in part because the national climate rendered it impractical to do otherwise, but it was also thanks to the growing notoriety of a speech delivered more than a decade prior by a Mississippi court justice by the name of Noah "Soggy" Sweat. This speech is worth including in its entirety because it sums up, with all the wistful poetry so typical of the Southern climes, the great shift in public opinion that redefined bourbon in the mid-twentieth century. And so, in a whimsical and no-doubt folksy drawl, we'll let the Honorable Judge "Soggy" take it away:

My friends, I had not intended to discuss this controversial subject at this particular time. However, I want you to know that I do not shun controversy. On the contrary, I will take a stand on any issue at any time, regardless of how fraught with controversy it might be. You have asked me how I feel about whiskey. All right, here is how I feel about whiskey.

If when you say "whiskey" you mean the devil's brew, the poison scourge, the bloody monster that defiles innocence, dethrones reason, destroys the home, creates misery and poverty, yea, literally takes the bread from the mouths of little children; if you mean the evil drink that topples the Christian man and woman from the pinnacle of righteous, gracious living into the bottomless pit of degradation, and despair, and shame, and helplessness, and hopelessness—then I am certainly against it.

But, if when you say "whiskey" you mean the oil of conversation, the philosophic wine, the ale that is consumed when good fellows get together, that puts a song in their hearts and laughter on their lips, and the warm glow of contentment in their eyes; if you mean Christmas cheer; if you mean the stimulating drink that puts the spring into the old gentleman's step on a frosty, crispy morning; if you mean the drink that enables a man to magnify his joy, and his happiness, and to forget, if only for a little while,

life's great tragedies, and heartaches, and sorrows;
if you mean that drink the sale of which pours into
our treasures untold millions of dollars, which are
used to provide tender care for our little crippled
children, our blind, our deaf, our dumb, our pitiful
aged and infirm; to build highways and hospitals
and schools—then certainly I am for it.

That is my stand. I will not retreat from it. I
will not compromise.

On that note, let's call it a night. It's almost suppertime, the missus is making that special meatloaf, and little Sally and Bobby are staying over at a friend's house. But not to worry. Bourbon and America are both in good hands. Cruising down the four-lane interstate highway of freedom, in an American-made Pontiac of progress, tossing the McDonald's containers of conformity in the backseat as we go, nothing can possibly go . . .

Wait, why's the new transmission making that grinding sound? And what are those freaky longhairs protesting by the side of the road? What's that awful noise coming from the radio? And why do those two pot-smoking hippies look so much like—oh my god! Sally! Bobby!

Can't believe it? Neither can bourbon. The times they are a-changing, all right, and this up-and-coming baby boom generation couldn't care less about keeping up with a bunch of squares like the Joneses. In fact, they don't want anything to do with a domestic, mass-produced whiskey that sold out for a few quick bucks and forgot its roots along the way. The distillers may have made a killing in the short term by appealing to suburban parents, but they've also alienated an entire generation in the process. And the American Spirit is about to become, in the pretentiously stilted parlance of the emerging young urban professional, officially *déclassé*.

9

It's a Small (Batch) World After All

HEDONISM, DECADENCE, PROFLIGACY, debauchery—such words may have made infrequent cameos in the Sunset Strip vernacular of the glam metal band Mötley Crüe, but as axiomatic principles, they were embraced as unquestionably and wholeheartedly as the ever-winking umlaut. Because to be a rock star was to push the boundaries of excess ever further, toward that self-fulfilling longitude—invisible, but mortally real—where glitter and doom became twinned on the horizon. Beneath the immoderate use of alcohol and narcotics lurked a lust for the Godhead, and for a bass player named Frank Carlton Serafino Ferranna Jr.—better known as Nikki Sixx—giving that Godhead a near-death noogie was simply the stuff of a Saturday night.

Now, bourbon and rock and roll had gone hand in hand long before leather pants and hairspray hit the scene. In fact, you might even say whiskey helped give birth to the rebellious spirit of rock music. According to some accounts, a young Elvis Presley moved to Memphis after his father got into trouble in Mississippi for using his company's delivery truck to drop off bootleg whiskey. Little Richard had a similar background—his old man was both a devout Seventh-Day Adventist and a law-bending bartender, famous for peddling illegal whiskey on the side. Jerry Lee Lewis also honed his image on a steady diet of whiskey and rebellion; rock and roll's first true wild man, he was getting loaded on bourbon and smashing hotel television sets (not to mention a few of his pianos) long before the Yardbirds or the Who showed up. And when the British Invasion did at last arrive, those shaggy-haired Englishmen weren't just imitating the rambunctious rhythms of American rock pioneers—they copied their drinking habits as well. Guitar legends like Keith Richards and Jimmy Page seldom missed an opportunity to be photographed with a bourbon bottle in hand, and some of their best gigs were played at the legendary L.A. club called, quite tellingly, the Whisky a Go Go.

It should come as no surprise then that Mötley Crüe liked their whiskey. And when it came to whiskey, they, like many rock bands of their era, were avid consumers of the Tennessee label Jack Daniel's. On the road, it was as easy to locate as willing young groupies, and thanks to the Lincoln County Process of smooth charcoal filtering, it was just as easy to party all night with. Nikki Sixx, along with his bandmates, sucked the stuff back like Coca-Cola,* giving it a starring role in nearly all of their shenanigans. Hotel orgies, tour bus bacchanals, strip club coke binges—one drunken Fourth of July party even resulted in a four-story palm tree being ignited by bottle rockets and toppling onto a vintage 1965 Mustang convertible. Such hijinks were commonplace, and fueled by the

---

* "Like milk" might be more accurate. The band confessed to putting Jack Daniel's in their Cap'n Crunch when the fridge was empty and they were too wasted to go to the store. As to whether the cereal stayed crunchy in whiskey, we simply don't know.

abuse of what had been a respectable and highly esteemed American whiskey.

That respect and esteem diminished even further, however, during the debacle that proved to be the Canadian leg of Mötley Crüe's 1987 tour. For in addition to alcohol, Nikki Sixx had by that point developed a severe dependency on heroin as well. Foreseeing potential problems in the scoring department—reliable heroin dealers were considerably harder to find than liquor stores—he had snuck a few grams of good Persian across the border along with his entourage. With a habit like his, however, those grams didn't go very far, and during one especially festive evening, Nikki and his bandmate/the future sex-tape star Tommy Lee found themselves with plenty of needles, but a troubling dearth of smack. At which point the two bandmates decided to take the codependent relationship between rock and roll and American whiskey to a disturbing new level. They made the joint decision to forgo the whole spoon and candle portion of the junkie ritual, as well as the shot glass and chaser part of the drinker's routine, and simply inject Jack Daniel's straight into their veins. The duo suctioned the amber-colored whiskey into their syringes, tied off, and shot up, in what was not only an incredibly dangerous breach of liquor protocol, human decency, and good sense, but also an incredibly stupid way to get drunk. "It didn't even occur to us that we could always just drink the JD," Tommy Lee would later recall. "Bro, let me tell you, there was something seriously wrong with us."

Nikki Sixx didn't die that night, although both he and bourbon whiskey would have their own share of near-death experiences over the course of this rocky decade. The rejection of American conformity that had begun under the guise of teenage rebelliousness and flower power in the late 1960s had gradually transformed into a full-blown disgust for any-

Like so many rock bands before them, Mötley Crüe enjoyed their whiskey.
A bottle of Jack even inspired the cover design of their memoir.

thing mass-produced and made in America by the 1980s, bourbon included. Tastes may have changed during the awkward transition from hippie to yuppie, but the distates did not, and the few people still willing to drink American whiskey were those unashamed of administering it solely as an intoxicant. Libertine frat boys, provincial alcoholics, skid-row barflies, self-destructive rock stars—bourbon's cheering section was hardly stellar and shrinking by the minute, as more and more baby boomers ditched the antiquated, corporate products of their parents for a fresh stream of flashy and seemingly foreign-made articles. Why would a prosperous young professional settle for rattletrap Chryslers and crappy Kraft Singles, when he could enjoy Swatches from Switzerland, Volvos from Sweden, Gucci loafers from Italy, and sashimi from Japan? Why would he gag back a glass of mundane bourbon, with its hokey labeling and total lack of umlauts, when he could easily pair his Häagen-Dazs with any number of French wines, craft beers, or trendy vodkas?

Good questions, and ones the bourbon industry found itself grappling with during the brand-conscious blossoming of Reagan's America. Outward-looking and freshly global, we as a nation felt entitled to stick up our noses at the bland, macro-produced world that had so enraptured us as a people a mere generation before. And the American Spirit suffered as a result. With bourbon's sales plummeting, and its reputation degraded practically to joke status, the whiskey that had nurtured a nation since day one found itself in very real danger of total irrelevance, if not extinction.

While corporate executives in the liquor industry pulled their hair and looked angst-ridden toward an uncertain future, a few of the older and wiser in the bourbon family knew that the key to their whiskey's continuance lay firmly rooted in its past. Under their careful watch, the American Spirit had survived revolutions, rebellions, and two pretty big world wars—they'd be damned if that legacy was going to be ruined by the likes of MTV and Marty McFly. If yuppies wanted carefully crafted items of luxury and class, then that's exactly what they were going to get. Bourbon may have sold out for some quick and easy sales in the glory days of the postwar years, but there were still a few among the old guard who remembered the old ways, and who hadn't forgotten how to make bourbon taste good. To live to see the twenty-first century, bourbon doesn't need to get bigger— it's already done that, only to become a victim of its own success. This time around, things are different, and for the first time in its entire existence, in order to survive, the American Spirit is going to have to get smaller.

ACCORDING TO THE Federal Standards of Identity for Distilled Spirits—a set of regulations whose origins can be found in the federal intervention bourbon distillers had lobbied for during the dark days of the Gilded Age—a whiskey may be sold as bourbon if it complies with a set list of criteria. First, it must come from a mash bill that contains at least 51 percent corn. Rye, barley, and sometimes wheat can figure into the grain mixture, but corn has to claim the majority. Second, the spirit must be distilled to no more than 160 proof, meaning it can't come out of the still higher than 80 percent alcohol. Third, it must spend some time aging in a new charred-oak barrel—there's no minimum age requirement, although to be sold as "straight" bourbon, which nearly all bourbons are, it needs to spend at least two years in the barrel, and not be mixed with any other additives. Fourth, it must enter the barrel at no higher than 125 proof, or 62.5 percent alcohol, and last, it cannot be bottled at anything lower than 80 proof, or 40 percent alcohol by volume.

If all of the above conditions are met, then any whiskey distiller operating on United States soil may proudly give birth to a brand-new baby bourbon*; any distiller who cannot adhere to them may not label its whiskey as such. Such rules had done the American bourbon industry a great service during the times when foul, rectified concoctions were still trying to pass themselves off as the real McCoy. During the corporate boom years following the Second World War, however, they had become something of a double-edged sword, for while they did maintain a minimal quality standard, they also didn't set the bar terribly high. A fairly flavorless and cringe-worthy whiskey could and very often did scrape by and still manage to sell itself as straight bourbon—when efficiency and mass production became the norm in the middle decades of the twentieth century, maximizing profits had often meant minimizing quality, with the taste of the whiskey diminishing as well. Gargantuan stainless steel vats replaced old cypress mash tubs; automated column stills pushed out the traditional copper; vast, climate-controlled rackhouses filled in for the dark and drafty barns of yore. The modern corporate distillery was able to churn out a tremendous amount of product at a minimized price, but it didn't take an expert distiller or whiskey connoisseur to tell you that something was different once the bottle was opened. Flat, flavorless, even harsh on the throat—this was not horribly rich or complex stuff. The rules of economics, however, simply did not care. The good folks in the head office saw no need to age bourbon for an entire decade, carefully rotating and sampling the barrels along the way, when that same whiskey could spend a couple of years in oak and get pushed out the door. Why bother? When bourbon went corporate, tradition and quality had begun to play second fiddle to the

---

* Contrary to what some may tell you, bourbon whiskey does not need to be made in Bourbon County, or even Kentucky, to be considered bourbon. It only has to be made in America. Hawaiian bourbon? It's theoretically possible. Puerto Rican bourbon? Well, that's up for debate.

primacy of profit. And the bourbon industry, like so many other American industries of the period, would come to pay the price once consumers caught on. "Made in the USA," formerly a signet of quality and pride, had become for many products a red letter of shame by the latter decades of the twentieth century. Detroit broke down, the Steel Belt rusted, and bourbon whiskey took a terrifying nosedive.

When did this disastrous plunge first start? Well, the thing about peaks is that they very often are tailed by the most precipitous of valleys, and bourbon proved to be no exception to the rule. A spirit's long-term success depends on a younger generation of drinkers picking up where aging drinkers leave off, and in the late '60s and early '70s, this simply was not happening. Amid the volatile social and political atmosphere surrounding events such as the Vietnam War, the civil rights movement, and the Watergate scandal, young Americans consciously—and in many cases, not without good cause—began rejecting conservative ideologies and cultural artifacts they associated with their parents and "the Establishment." And unfortunately for bourbon, after two decades of spirituous hegemony in the American psyche, its oak-aged amber tincture was about as established as any drink could get. Full of yearnings for peace, love, and transcendence, the hippies came of age on marijuana and psychedelics, leaving the brown stuff to those who LSD guru Timothy Leary labeled as "middle-aged, middle-class, whiskey-drinking, bluenosed bureaucrats." When sandals turned to platform shoes in the vapid disco years that followed, flavorless and cocktail-friendly vodka took over, surpassing whiskey as America's drink of choice around the time our nation celebrated its bicentennial.* And by

---

* Adding insult to injury, a tornado struck one of Jim Beam's distilleries on April 3, 1974, destroying a six-story aging warehouse and sending more than 5,200 barrels of bourbon swirling into the sky. It was a sad day for bourbon . . . but a great day for the residents of Oz.

the *me, me, me* years of the 1980s, bourbon was a mere shadow of what it had once been—older drinkers stuck to fine wines and expensive single malt scotches, while younger revelers preferred their Cokes rummy and their tonics well-vodkanated.

After twenty postwar years at the top of the booze chain, oh, how the mighty bourbon had fallen. In the final peak year of 1970, almost eighty-five million gallons of bourbon were sold; by 1983, Kentucky distilleries were struggling to turn out a mere fifty million gallons, augmented only in the most meager of fashions by the handful of distilleries scattered across nearby states. Layoffs ensued, several distilleries shut down, and frantic board meetings were held, as top executives desperately sought a solution to a seemingly insolvable problem: How can we make bourbon respectable again?

Some brands were in denial about the bourbon generation gap that was crippling their sales.

Alas, while the bigwigs banged their heads and explored all sorts of diversification tactics and modernization methods, a few of the old-timers couldn't help but wonder if the answer wasn't sitting right there, traditionally made and carefully crafted, beneath their very own noses. Which brings us to a couple of interesting fellows whose bourbon pedigree stretches back to the earliest days of barrel-aged corn liquor, and whose taste for good whiskey was never hampered by sales data or market trends. It's time to meet two of the small batch movement's founding fathers: Bill Samuels and Booker Noe.

TODAY, THE NOTION that crafting goods in smaller quantities, using better-quality ingredients and time-tested production methods, will result in a more desirable product may seem quaintly intuitive. But in the mass-produced, better-living-through-chemistry world that arrived in the wake of the Second World War, such ideas were at best preposterous, and at worst un-American. Which is precisely why when Bill Samuels Sr. unveiled his new Maker's Mark whiskey in the fall of 1959, more than a few of his competitors scoffed at its arrival. Oh, he had the background all right, coming from one of Kentucky's oldest bourbon-making families, and he definitely knew his way around a mash tub—his grandfather T. W. Samuels had opened a distillery way back in 1844. But the ideas he proposed were simply beyond the pale. He was more of a hobbyist or tinkerer than a profit-minded entrepreneur, and his bourbon was the product of some fairly nonconventional thinking for that time. For starters, he used wheat* instead of the standard rye as a flavoring grain, in an

---

* How did Bill Samuels Sr. find the perfect grain combinations? According to his son Bill Samuels Jr., it was not in the distillery or gristmill, but in the kitchen—baking bread.

effort to give his whiskey a smoother finish—a technique that had been experimented with at George Washington's Mount Vernon distillery almost two centuries before. Something of a traditionalist, he also rejected the notion of building some flashy new state-of-the-art plant, insisting instead on producing his Maker's Mark on the foundations of an old gristmill distillery built in the early 1800s. And last, he was of the strong opinion that bourbon could be a high-quality product, and ought to be sold as such. With a little help from his wife, he devised the clever gimmick of dipping each bottle in wax to create a seal; "It tastes expensive," went his now-famous marketing slogan, "and is."

The idea was brilliant . . . but also about two decades ahead of its time. And sales, those tricky little figures so dependent on the wants and whims of a fickle public, were impeded for that very reason. Undeterred, however, the Samuelses pushed on with unwavering conviction, telling all who would listen that their bourbon was made in small quantities, using traditional methods, and, unlike much of its far less expensive competition, was actually pleasurable to drink. None of which did much good. The America of the '60s and '70s just wasn't interested in a high-quality, top-shelf bourbon. The idea seemed as absurd as a $200 pair of designer blue jeans, as ridiculous as a burger made from Kobe beef.

Not that Maker's Mark was totally without willing customers. One of the more astute and innovative marketing schemes the Samuels family came up with was to get their whiskey on the beverage carts of airplanes and in the pages of airline magazines—because on board a 747, a lesser-known bourbon label like Maker's had a captive, upwardly mobile audience of professionals looking for novel ways to kill the boredom of a long flight. A high-class, expensive-tasting Kentucky bourbon? Sure, why not? It certainly sounded strange, but with nothing to do at thirty thousand feet, jet-setters were willing to try just

Close to home: the refurbished Maker's Mark distillery in Loretto, Kentucky.

about anything. The strategy wasn't enough to make any mountains out of sales charts, but it did help to keep the young brand in business, as well as garner the attention of a few folks interested in bright ideas and new marketing trends.

Like the *Wall Street Journal*, for example. Word was indeed getting around, and on August 1, 1980, the *Journal* published a front-page article on a true Kentucky curiosity, alerting the general drinking and investing public to the following peculiarities:

> *Maker's Mark Distillery has made its mark by*
> *going against the grain. In producing its premium-*
> *priced Maker's Mark bourbon, it continues to*
> *use an intricate six-year aging process and a small*
> *bottling line that are models of inefficiency. It*
> *distills only 19 barrels of bourbon daily, compared*
> *with hundreds distilled by other producers. Its ad*
> *budget is a meager $1.2 million a year. But most*
> *remarkably, its volume of business has more than*
> *tripled, to about 150,000 cases a year, in the past*
> *10 years, while the bourbon industry's sales have*
> *slipped 26%, to 23.7 million.*

Bourbon-savvy readers surely absorbed those words with their curiosity fully piqued, because at that point, while the rest of the bourbon industry had seen its sales slip by more than a quarter over the course of a catastrophic decade, this strange little Maker's Mark brand was quietly puttering along and slowly growing its consumer base. Slowly growing prior to the article, anyway. After its publication, the brand suddenly had America's attention. Because in 1980, yuppie culture was just beginning to blossom. A renewed interest in gourmet food and fine wines was germinating, not to mention a hunger for premium, artisanal goods.* Maker's Mark was no longer ahead of its time, but rather right on the cusp

---

* Interestingly enough, the renewed interest in fine wine and haute cuisine that America experienced in the 1980s—and that reinvigorated the bourbon industry—can be attributed to none other than Julia Child. So thank her and your local PBS station next time you crack the red wax seal on a bottle of Maker's.

of a paradigm shift in American culture. After more than twenty years of marketplace irrelevance, its values and those of American drinkers had at last aligned. And sales, which had been growing previously at only a modest rate, took off like F-14 Tomcats behind the *Wall Street Journal* article's slipstream.

Bourbon at large, however, had a long way to go. General sales were still declining, the public still wasn't totally sold on the idea that whiskey could be classy, and other spirits were still edging it off of bar shelves across the country. But people in the industry did take notice, and a few were even willing to try something new. In 1984, the Ancient Age Distillery—today known as Buffalo Trace Distillery—took the bold step of introducing a single barrel bourbon called Blanton's, making it the nation's first superpremium straight bourbon since Prohibition's repeal. Sales were initially modest, but it got people talking, and it put a top-notch luxury bourbon right up alongside the expensive European liquors that were beginning to appear in America's classier drinking establishments and eateries. Could whiskey, for so long the provenance of outdated Kentucky gentlemen, old granddads, and some pretty wild turkeys, finally shed its economy-class baggage and join Monsieur Cognac and good Sir Scotch in their first-class seats?

Why the heck not. That surely was the sentiment of more than a few of the hereditary distillers in bourbon country. After all, Scotland had done it. The British recession of the 1970s had left a glut of scotch aging in Caledonian distilleries; when their traditional markets at the big blended labels said "nae, thank ye" in the '80s, those wise Highlanders and Islanders re-marketed their local products across the pond as premium single malts, just in time for the young urban professionals' Reagan-era version of cocktail hour. And not to be outdone by foreigners, domestic beer had executed a similar about-face in the PR department, spurred by the success of trendy new microbrewer-

It
tastes
expensive
...and is.

Maker's Mark

Made from an original old style sour mash recipe by Bill Samuels, fourth generation Kentucky Distiller.

Also available in Limited Edition 101 proof

Maker's Mark was among the first to present bourbon as an upscale drink.

ies like Samuel Adams (founded in 1984). If other plebian potations could clean up their image and reinvent themselves as luxury goods, there seemed few impediments to bourbon following a similar course. All that was required was a singular man with the knowledge, wisdom, and temerity to do so.

Meet Booker Noe. And don't let the surname fool you—it may sound inconsequential enough, but the man was a Beam, Jim's grandson in fact, making him a certified member of one of the oldest and most celebrated bourbon families to ever cross the Appalachians and set up a still. In charge of the company's Boston plant for nearly forty years, he was responsible for the brand's meteoric rise in the second half of the twentieth century, and in many ways its savior when things got rocky toward the century's end. Most of the premium bourbons we know today were either directly born or indirectly inspired by an innovation of his that turned out to be not much of an innovation at all—in the end, Booker Noe stuck to what he knew and what he believed in, and as with Maker's Mark, America eventually caught up. Or perhaps more accurately, came around again.

So just what was this bourbon innovation? Well, spend enough time with any master distiller, and sooner or later, he's likely to show you his private stash. For men like Jimmy Russell at Wild Turkey, Parker Beam at Heaven Hill, Lincoln Henderson at Early Times, Elmer T. Lee at Ancient Age, and yes, Booker Noe at Jim Beam, bourbon whiskey was a high art. And no true artist can let a masterpiece go to waste. Accordingly, when an especially fine barrel of bourbon came along, it was not unusual to single it out, set it quietly aside, perhaps let it age a little longer than usual, and when the time was right, bottle it up for private consumption. For among the many perks of being a distiller, few were as pleasurable as having unfettered access to some of the finest whiskey in the world. Mr. Noe was known to be especially fond of his personal "Booker's Bourbon," even offering a sample of the small batch elixir to a *Chicago Tribune* reporter as early as 1974—its aroma was so rich, she could smell it across the room. Among cherished employees, old friends, and distinguished guests, Booker's special bourbon quickly became legendary.

But it was never sold. For much of the master distiller's career, there simply had been no market for a carefully crafted small batch bourbon, worthy of being sipped from a snifter like the finest of cognacs. Complex flavors, ephemeral bouquets, hints of toasted almond, citrus, and honeysuckle—such things had simply never been sought by the American

Yes, you might say bourbon had an image problem.

consumer. Sure, the rare connoisseur or master distiller knew quality could exist in bourbon and ought to be savored, but for the average Joe plopping on a barstool or dropping by the liquor store, bourbon was expected to be cheap, simple, and eminently mixable. Heck, he probably had never held a snifter in his life.

By 1987, however, the American palate was beginning to change. When Barry Berish, the president of Jim Beam, requested ideas for a unique holiday gift to be passed along to the company's key distributors, a sales manager by the name of Michael Donohoe thought back to his own private drinking sessions with Booker Noe, and the distiller's special whiskey instantly came to mind—a one-of-a-kind private stock bourbon that liquor magnates could proudly put beside their rarest single malts. Using old Chablis bottles that had been collecting dust in a warehouse, and attaching a note to each handwritten by Booker himself, they carefully prepared a few hundred of the tantalizing presents, using uncut, unfiltered whiskey from only the choicest of barrels.

The reaction was immediate. No sooner had the corks been popped than the calls poured in, as distributors and vendors sought to discover how they could get their hands on more bottles of "Booker's Bourbon" and sell it to their own patrons. Encouraged by the overwhelmingly positive response, Booker Noe and Michael Donohoe sprang into action, and just one year later, in 1988, the first public batch of one thousand six-bottle cases of Booker's Bourbon were released to the world, accompanied by much fanfare and rave reviews. With Maker's Mark, America had rediscovered that bourbon could taste good; with Booker's, the country learned once again that bourbon could be an art form.

What made Booker's Bourbon so special? As previously mentioned, it was neither cut with water nor filtered, giving it a rustic purity that harkened back to the robust Kentucky whiskeys of yore. But perhaps more important, it was the selection of prime extra-aged barrels that set it apart. In Booker's own words:

> *What I'm hunting for are the barrels in the center rows [of the rackhouse], the fifth and sixth stories.*

*The "center cut" is what I call them. . . . I select
from these central areas because I know from
experience that the whiskeys in the seven to eight
year range will be oaky and vanilla-like, robust
but smooth. Not too much tannin, but lots of
texture. Too much tannin will have it taste too dry,
overdone. I like Booker's to be on the sweeter side.
Hell, think of the center cut from a watermelon,
that sweetest part. Center cut's what it's all about
for Booker's.*

By carefully choosing barrels from the same age group, and from the same portion of the rackhouse, Booker was able to turn out an undiluted, unfiltered small batch whiskey unlike anything seen in generations—a total anachronism, and a delicious one at that. And lucky for him, and for all of us, America was finally ready to rediscover its spirit. Booker's success helped launch a small batch revolution in the bourbon world, as label after label released its own unique interpretation of what fine bourbon should be. Four Roses, Heaven Hill, Evan Williams, Jack Daniel's—they would all craft their own premium labels during the bourbon renaissance years of the late '80s and '90s. And following the lucky strike Jim Beam had experienced with Booker's, that premium offering was soon augmented by an entire small batch collection. By the mid-'90s, the company could claim some of the biggest small batch names in the business, including Knob Creek (named after the Kentucky stream that trickled past Abe Lincoln's childhood home), Basil Hayden's, and Baker's.

The great fanfare and general enthusiasm that attended the rise of small batch and single barrel bourbons through the decade of the 1990s became increasingly tinged—if not flat-out fueled—by a mounting nostalgia for a time, real or not, when things were just plain simpler. With the rise of cyber-space, and the increasing digitization of everyday life, it is perhaps not surprising that the thirst for premium liquors would gradually morph, as the twentieth century came to a close, into a longing for something that had been lost in the postmodern hubbub. When the future appears so profoundly uncertain, it's only natural for a people to reconnect with tradition.

The arrival of Woodford Reserve in 1996 was arguably the pinnacle of the small batch movement. Founded on the very site where Elijah Pepper and Dr. James C. Crow once turned fine bourbon into an American institution, and owned by the same Brown-Forman company that George Garvin Brown had established to bring bottled integrity to our national drink, the distillery restored the original stone structures and implemented traditional copper pot stills to make high-quality whiskey almost exactly as it was done more than a century ago. In rediscovering the old and meld-

History repeats itself: the traditional pot stills
and stone masonry at Woodford Reserve.

ing it with the new, a venerable tradition of small batch distilling that had essentially been relegated to the history books was resurrected; among the verdant hills and sprawling horse farms of central Kentucky, an old distillery was reborn, and with it, fresh hope and a new direction for the American Spirit.

WHEN THE NEW millennium did come around, those fears of bourbon's inevitable demise left over from the '70s and early '80s proved to be as unfounded as that whole Y2K nonsense. Bourbon didn't just survive—it took off, entering the twenty-first century with an irrefutable bang. Between 2002 and 2006, sales of bourbon (including Tennessee whiskey) rose by a solid 12.23 percent; during that same period, sales of high-end whiskeys shot up by 27.62 percent, and sales of superpremium bourbons skyrocketed by an incredible 60.52 percent. In the year that followed, overall bourbon exports would also see sizable growth, jumping from $623 million to $713 million, bolstered by a growing demand abroad for the finest whiskeys that America had to offer. And for the entire first decade of the twenty-first century, bourbon production would increase by more than 50 percent—unequivocal evidence that those who had bet against the American Spirit, from the Bolsheviks all the way up to Bin Laden, had most definitely put their money on the wrong horse at the Kentucky Derby.

So, for those readers who shut their eyes and clamped their ears as the baby boom generation transitioned from hippies to yuppies, casting aside bourbon along with their station wagons and worn-out phonographs, you can relax. In America, you can go home again, and in our wanderings and meanderings, we may stray from the path, but we're never too far from where we began. In our collective tale, there's always room for a little redemption, and if members of a big-haired rock band can shoot whiskey into their veins without giving up the ghost, surely our spirit can survive an overdose or two of misguided notions and questionable taste, and still come out blazing in the end. Without such dips and dabbles, the impetus never would have existed to bring bourbon back to its rightful place among the great whiskeys and fine liquors of the world. Just as the repentant glam rocker will tell you during his cable-televised confessional—you've got to hit rock bottom before you can climb your way back up to the top.

EPILOGUE

Bourbon Renewal

To VISIT TUTHILLTOWN in high season is to take a heady step into bourbon's rich past. Girdled by soft hills and bee-combed copses, surrounded by quiet fields of corn and rye, situated on the site of a gristmill that churned for more than two centuries, the distillery is nestled within a fine country for making whiskey. Corn dust, freshly milled, stirs in the air; mash tubs burble steadily, sweetly redolent of malt and yeast; when summoned, the copper stills tremble most fervently to life. Workers chat as they carefully hammer corks into the tops of finished bottles, and the glass clinks and chimes while being loaded into cases, bound for destinations far across the hills. It's enough to make a bourbon aficionado close his eyes and breathe in deeply of that sweet Kentucky air. . . .

Only, that bourbon aficionado may be in for a pulmonary shock, because Tuthilltown Spirits isn't in Kentucky—or even Tennessee, for that matter. The distillery is located in Gardiner, New York, and has borne the proud mantle since its founding in 2003 of being the state's first legal distillery to open since Prohibition. Its Hudson Baby Bourbon Whiskey picks up where a tradition of local craft distilling left off nearly a century before, and invokes an era when small-scale whiskey making was a part of everyday rural and frontier life across America, to be found wherever grain and stills might peacefully coexist. And since bourbon need not be from Kentucky, its oak-aged corn liquor can make the same rightful claim to the title as any distillery puffing away in the Bluegrass. Like the gray wolf returning to Yellowstone, or the bald eagle once again swooping down upon the lower forty-eight states, American whiskey has begun to reclaim its native range. This has not transpired as part of any large-scale corporate takeover, but rather in the sort of small, local, and folksy increments that put American whiskey on the map in the first place. Using largely locally produced organic grain, traditional techniques, and old-fashioned pot stills, the micro-distillery movement has seen highly respected craft bourbons crop up in California, Oregon, Virginia, Texas—there's even a bourbon distillery in Brooklyn, and with an establishment date of 2010, it can officially boast of being New York City's oldest *operating* whiskey distillery—and quite a boast it is, in a city whose distilling legacy stretches back to the 1640s, when the Dutch held dominion and it was known as New Amsterdam.

Far from being a solely alcoholic phenomenon, the recent reemergence of traditional, locally sourced crafts can be seen as part of a larger cultural trend that first gained a foothold in the early aughts. Marked by a longing for a sense of true "authenticity," it has compelled a new generation of younger Americans to actively seek out a moral and aesthetic sensibility that draws heavily from the shared memory of the American past. This predilection has become apparent in clothing styles, food choices, musical tastes, and yes, even beverage selection. Essentially, as a people, we've gained enough cultural distance from our folkloric ancestors to make that world seem cool again. Reality television crackles with tales of backwoods moonshiners, NPR hums with bluegrass festivals, J.Crew and Ralph Lauren urge sophisticated urbanites to dress like Depression-era stevedores, and in the midst of all of it, bourbon has gained a cultural currency never seen before. For the better part of our history, Americans drank it because with its availability and low cost, they didn't have much choice. Today, it's increasingly sought out and imbibed as a means of communion with that very past. Because for a people actively searching out what is real and worth preserving in their heritage, bourbon is understandably seen to be as real as it gets—and if it's made right, it's a piece of our past that tastes pretty good, too. At the root of our nation's current bourbon renaissance, and manifested in the clusters of craft distilleries that are sprouting directly from it, one can readily detect the most basic of needs—a sense of identity, place, and belonging.

But wait one second, the observant reader is almost certainly interjecting, rightfully skeptical after having been treated to three roller-coaster centuries of America's fickle vicissitudes. Isn't it possible that the craft and microdistillery trend, with its contrived authenticity and hints of ironic hipsterdom, is just one more of the many fads that have buoyed and sunk bourbon over the many years? A fair point of contention, to which one can answer: almost certainly. The American Spirit never has been and never will be a static enterprise. But as we have seen over the course of this jaunty trek through the rackhouse of time, while the strength of that spirit has gained a great deal from tradition, it has gained even more from the rich diversity of its own experience. And a short step back to take a more encompassing gander at today's bourbon landscape reveals an experience that is as rich and diverse as ever. While a micro-distillery might labor heroically to turn out a few hundred bottles of high-end artisanal whiskey a month for local consumption, Jim Beam's single J line can turn out three hundred bottles a minute, and sends its millions of annual cases to the far corners of the globe. While fashionable restaurants in New York City and Los Angeles serve bourbon-inspired gourmet tasting menus to celebrities and glitterati, down-home saloons and honky-tonks across our hinterlands still serve comfort from a jukebox and camaraderie by the shot glass. While the international conglomerates that own the major bourbon labels include such cosmopolitan titles as Kirin, Diageo, and Sazerac, the roster of master distillers is still dominated by the same twangy surnames that crossed the Appalachians alongside Daniel Boone. And while Kentucky currently has more barrels of aging bourbon within its borders than it does people—close to five million, as a matter of fact—even that doesn't seem to be enough. Maker's Mark nearly caused a riot in 2013 when it announced (and then quickly backpedaled on) a plan to water down its whiskey to keep up with demand, and if you want a bottle of Pappy Van Winkle's Family Reserve, good luck finding one—they're going on eBay for hundreds of dollars.

Only in America, perhaps, is such a diversity of experience possible, and as long as it remains possible, the integrity of our spirit shall remain robust and solidly intact. The flame George Thorpe brought to life all those centuries ago on the quivering edge of a great and promising continent was fragile indeed, but also surprisingly resilient; it stayed lit through a litany of wars, massacres, and all manner of revolutions by bending quite admirably to the winds of time—bending, yet never ceasing to burn.

The American Spirit taking its rightful place at the table.

All of which presents your Faithful Author with the final challenge of bringing to a satisfactory close a story that here, in the adolescent years of a new twenty-first century, is really only just beginning—a daunting curtain call, to say the least.

He did consider mentioning how all of those used bourbon barrels from Kentucky are being shipped across the sea to Europe for the aging of scotch, completing a transatlantic cultural circle that began with the discovery of the New World. As it turns out, the distilleries of Kentucky and those of Scotland have developed a mutually beneficial partnership over the years. Due to the federal regulations mentioned previously, bourbon must be made from *new* oak barrels—meaning there is a tremendous quantity of used barrels with no obvious use in America. Back in Scotland, however, where the roots of American whiskey lie, no such barrel restrictions exist for their native spirit. In fact, the distillers of single malts, who happen to have some of the keenest noses and tongues in the world, prefer their scotch to be aged in bourbon barrels; they find it brings a richness and complexity to their fine whiskey that's otherwise unattainable. Not a bad finish, for a book or a bourbon barrel.

He also considered going out on a note of literary poignancy, including a favorite passage from a bourbon-loving author about the past not even being past yet, or with America beating on ceaselessly against currents—something like that. Bourbon has held such a pivotal role in our nation's culture, there's almost no end to the analogies and anecdotes to be drawn from it. It has appeared again and again across artistic genres, featured prominently in book passages, song lyrics, and film scenes of every sort. From hard-drinking novelists to hard-boiled detectives, Hollywood cowboys to *National Lampoon*'s fraternity boys, bourbon's champions cover the gamut of the American experience. There's no shortage of material to pull from, and no end to the list of great bourbon-inspired lines and scenes that might lend to a final chapter a meaningful sense of closure.

He even considered finishing on a personal note, and relating how much he has enjoyed drinking homemade whiskey while visiting his family's farm, made by his cousin from corn grown on some of the same fields his father and grandfather had once plowed and planted. Poured from an old glass decanter, and enjoyed in a chipped coffee mug alongside a healthy plug of chaw, it's pretty strong stuff— moonshine, really. The fumes alone can provoke a cough, and certainly have on more than one occasion. But each sip, however bracing, is a potent reminder of how and where the American Spirit began: not in an air-conditioned boardroom or a corporate-owned factory, but on a family

Your Faithful Author (left) drinking homemade whiskey with his cousin Garland.

farm hacked out of the wilderness, the fruits of honest labor and leftover grain.

Any one of these endings would surely have sufficed. But given the turbulence and chop America has already experienced during the first small portion of this new century, and the many challenges and hurdles that no doubt lie ahead, it is perhaps most fitting to simply close with a practical bit of wisdom from a bourbon drinker by the name of Lyndon B. Johnson.

Here it goes:

> *Now we may have more preachers out there than we have drinkers. But a fellow told a story one time about a man down in Kentucky, where they make bourbon. And he said you can take a jigger or maybe two jiggers and get by all right. But if you try to take the whole bottle, why you have lost what you started with. So don't try to take it too quick. And don't try to do all of it at once. . . . I don't do much promising. I tell what my goals are and then I try to wrap it up and put a blue ribbon on it and get it delivered. We say put the coonskin on the wall— that's what counts.*

Don't try to take the whole bottle at once—wise words for politicians, citizens, and writers alike. Because the American Spirit's best stories are still to be told, and its greatest chapters have yet to be written. Who knows what the future may hold? Bourbon on the moon rocks? Kegs in space? Drunk Rogers in the twenty-fifth century? Only time will tell.

So enough preaching already.

Who's ready to go get a drink?

Acknowledgments

I OWE A HEARTFELT thank-you to my agent, Jim Fitzgerald, for suggesting this book; my editor, Peter Hubbard, and his assistant, Cole Hager, for enabling it to come to life; and *ma petite* Sophie for being patient with me while I wrote it. I would also like to express my gratitude to Dennis Pogue and the Mount Vernon Ladies' Association for sending me in the right direction, the National Archives for their numerous photocopies, and Bill Samuels Jr. for giving the manuscript an early read. And naturally, a tremendous thanks to my parents for their ongoing love and support—I owe you both far more than any acknowledgment can properly express.

And last, I'd like to thank my liver for bearing with me through those long months of grueling "research." Sorry, little buddy. But it was worth it.

Bibliography

PROLOGUE: AMERICA IN A BOTTLE
CHAPTER 1: CATALANS, CORN BEER, AND THE AGE OF DISCOVERY

Meece, Mickey. "Bourbon's All-American Roar." *New York Times*, December 24, 2011.

Jones, David. "U.S. Whiskey Makers Look Abroad for Spirited Growth." Reuters, October 9, 2009.

Bonner, Anthony. "Historical Background and Life" (an annotated *Vita Coaetanea*) in Bonner (ed.), *Doctor Illuminatus*. Princeton: Princeton University Press, 1985.

Bonner, Anthony. *Selected Works of Ramon Llull (1232–1316)*. Princeton: Princeton University Press, 1985.

Forbes, R. J. *A Short History of the Art of Distillation*. Leiden: E. J. Brill, 1948.

Coe, Sophie. *America's First Cuisines*. Austin: University of Texas Press, 1994.

Waldman, Carl. *Atlas of the North American Indian*. 3rd ed. Checkmate Books, 2009.

Smith, Wayne, Javier Betran, and E. C. A. Runge. *Corn: Origin, History, Technology, and Production*. Hoboken, NJ: John Wiley & Sons, 2004.

CHAPTER 2: A TALE OF TWO GEORGES

Puleo, Stephen. *Dark Tide: The Great Boston Molasses Flood of 1919*. Boston: Beacon Press, 2003.

Neill, Edward. "Massacre at Falling Creek, Virginia." *Magazine of American History with Notes and Queries*, vol. 1. New York and Chicago: A. S. Barnes & Company, 1877.

5th Report of the Royal Commission on Historical Manuscripts. Pt. 1. London: George and Edward Eyre and William Spottiswoode, Printers to the Queen's Most Excellent Majesty, 1876.

Geith-Jones, Eric. *George Thorpe and the Berkely Company*. Gloucester: Alan Sutton Publishing, 1982.

Williams, Ian. *Rum: A Social and Sociable History*. New York: Nation Books, 2005.

Rorabaugh, W. J. *The Alcoholic Republic: An American Tradition*. New York: Oxford University Press, 1979.

Pogue, Dennis. *Founding Spirits: George Washington and the Beginnings of the American Whiskey Industry*. Buena Vista, VA: Harbour Books, 2011.

Twohig, Dorothy. *The Papers of George Washington: Presidential Series*. Charlottesville: University of Virginia Press, 1987.

CHAPTER 3: THE SCOTS-IRISH ARE COMING,
THE SCOTS-IRISH ARE COMING!

Rice, Otis. *The Hatfields and the McCoys*. Lexington: University of Kentucky Press, 1982.

MacAdam, Robert, ed. "On the Early Uses of Aqua-Vitae in Ireland." *Ulster Journal of Archaeology*. Belfast: Archer & Sons, 1858.

Rohrbough, Malcolm. *Trans-Appalachian Frontier: People, Societies, and Institutions*. 3rd ed. Bloomington: Indiana University Press, 2008.

Hackett Fischer, David. *Albion's Seed: Four British Folkways in America*. New York: Oxford University Press, 1989.

McCarthy, Karen. *The Other Irish: The Scots-Irish Rascals That Made America*. New York: Sterling, 2011.

Hoefling, Larry. *Chasing the Frontier: Scots-Irish in Early America*. Lincoln: iUniverse, 2005.

Webb, Jim. *Born Fighting: How the Scots-Irish Shaped America*. New York: Broadway Books, 2004.

Pogue, Dennis. *Founding Spirits: George Washington and the Beginnings of the American Whiskey Industry*. Buena Vista, VA: Harbour Books, 2011.

Hall, Harrison. *The Distiller*. Philadelphia: Printed by J. Bioren, 1818.

Crowgey, Henry. *Kentucky Bourbon: The Early Days of Whiskeymaking*. Lexington: University of Kentucky Press, 2008.

Rorabaugh, W. J. *The Alcoholic Republic: An American Tradition*. New York: Oxford University Press, 1979.

CHAPTER 4: BOURBON'S REBELLIOUS PHASE

Schroeder-Lein, Glenna. *The Encyclopedia of Civil War Medicine*. Armonk, NY: M. E. Sharp, 2008.

Brinton, John. *Personal Memoirs of John H. Brinton*. New York: Neale Publishing Company, 1914.

Pogue, Dennis. *Founding Spirits: George Washington and the Beginnings of the American Whiskey Industry*. Buena Vista, VA: Harbour Books, 2011.

Sherman, William. *Sherman: Memoirs of General W. T. Sherman*. New York: Literary Classics of the United States, 1990.

Parker, Thomas. *History of the 51st Regiment of P.V. and V.V.* Philadelphia: King & Baird, 1869.

Carson, Gerald. *The Social History of Bourbon.* Lexington: University of Kentucky Press, 1963.

Holzheuter, John. "William Wallace's Civil War Letters: The Virginia Campaign." *Wisconsin Magazine of History,* vol. 57, no. 1 (autumn 1973).

Lowry, Thomas. *Irish and German, Whiskey and Beer: Drinking Patterns in the Civil War.* Lexington: self-published, 2011.

Harper's Weekly: A Journal of Civilization, vol. 6, February 22, 1862.

Gately, Iain. *Drink: A Cultural History of Alcohol.* New York: Gotham Books, 2009.

Jones, J. William. *Personal Reminiscences, Anecdotes, and Letters of Gen. Robert E. Lee.* New York: D. Appleton and Company, 1875.

Riley, Elihu. *Stonewall Jackson: A Thesaurus of Anecdotes of and Incidents in the Life of Lieut-General Thomas Jonathan Jackson, C.S.A.* Annapolis: Riley Historical Series, 1920.

Tanner, Robert. *Stonewall in the Valley: Thomas J. "Stonewall" Jackson's Shenandoah Valley Campaign, Spring 1862.* Mechanicsburg, PA: Stackpole Books, 1996.

Jackson, Mary Anna. *Life and Letters of General Thomas J. Jackson (Stonewall Jackson).* New York: Harper & Brothers, 1892.

Peck, Rufus: *Reminiscences of a Confederate Soldier of Company C, 2nd Virginia Cavalry.* Fincastle, VA: privately published, 1913.

Bernard, George. *Civil War Talks: Further Reminiscences of George S. Bernard and His Fellow Veterans.* Charlottesville: University of Virginia Press, 2012.

James, Terry. *Lee's Tigers: The Louisiana Infantry in the Army of Northern Virginia.* Baton Rouge: Louisiana State University Press, 1987.

Dufour, Charles. *Gentle Tiger: The Gallant Life of Roberdeau Wheat.* Baton Rouge: Louisiana State University Press, 1957.

Mingus, Scott. *The Louisiana Tigers in the Gettysburg Campaign.* Baton Rouge: Louisiana State University Press, 2009.

Samuels, Bill, Jr. *Maker's Mark: My Autobiography.* Louisville: Saber Publishing, 2000.

Pacult, Paul. *American Still Life: The Jim Beam Story and the Making of the World's #1 Bourbon.* Hoboken, NJ: John Wiley & Sons, 2003.

Krass, Peter. *Blood and Whiskey: The Life and Times of Jack Daniel.* Hoboken, NJ: John Wiley & Sons, 2004.

CHAPTER 5: WHISKEY FROM A GILDED GLASS

Scharf, J. Thomas. *A History of St. Louis City and County, from the Earliest Periods to the Present Day.* Philadelphia: L. H. Everts & Company, 1883.

Rives, Timothy. "Grant, Babcock, and the Whiskey Ring." *Prologue: Quarterly of the National Archives and Records Administration,* vol. 32, no. 3 (fall 2000).

McDonald, John. *Secrets of the Great Whiskey Ring and Eighteen Months in the Penitentiary*. St. Louis: W. S. Bryan, 1880.

Crowgey, Henry. *Kentucky Bourbon: The Early Days of Whiskeymaking*. Lexington: University of Kentucky Press, 2008.

Pogue, Dennis. *Founding Spirits: George Washington and the Beginnings of the American Whiskey Industry*. Buena Vista, VA: Harbour Books, 2011.

Hall, Harrison. *The Distiller*. Philadelphia: Printed by J. Bioren, 1818.

Klein, Maury. *The Genesis of Industrial America, 1870–1920*. New York: Cambridge University Press, 2007.

Cashman, Sean. *America in the Gilded Age: From the Death of Lincoln to the Rise of Theodore Roosevelt*. New York: New York University Press, 1993.

Monzert, Leonard. *Leonard Monzert's Practical Distiller*. New York: Dick & Fitzgerald, 1889.

Boynton, H. V. "The Whiskey Ring." *North American Review,* vol. 123, no. 253 (October 1876).

Internal Revue Record and Customs Journal, vol. 29. New York: W. C. & F. P. Church, Publishers, 1883.

"Bourbon Whisky Trust. Kentucky Distillers Will Oppose the American Spirits Company." *New York Times*, February 12, 1897.

CHAPTER 6: HOW THE WEST WAS FUN

Reasoner, James. *Draw: The Greatest Gunfights of the American West*. New York: Berkley Books, 2003.

"Fort Worth's White Elephant Saloon." *Wild West Magazine*, June 12, 2006.

Twain, Mark. *Life on the Mississippi*. New York: Grosset & Dunlap, 1917.

Erdoes, Richard. *Saloons of the Old West*. New York: Gramercy Books, 1997.

Martin, Cy. *Whiskey and Wild Women: An Amusing Account of the Saloons and Bawds of the Old West*. New York: Hart Publishing, 1974.

Abbott, E. C. *We Pointed Them North: Recollections of a Cowpuncher*. Norman: University of Oklahoma Press, 1955.

Gately, Iain. *Drink: A Cultural History of Alcohol*. New York: Gotham Books, 2009.

Carson, Gerald. *The Social History of Bourbon*. Lexington: University of Kentucky Press, 1963.

West, Elliott. *The Saloons of the Rocky Mountain Mining Frontier*. Lincoln: University of Kentucky Press, 1979.

Klein, Maury. *The Genesis of Industrial America, 1870–1920*. New York: Cambridge University Press, 2007.

Rosa, Joseph, and Robin May. *Gunlaw: A Study of Violence in the Wild West*. Contemporary Books, 1977.

Masterson, W. B. *Famous Gunfighters of the Western Frontier*. Mineola, NY: Dover Publications, 2009.

CHAPTER 7: AN IRISHMAN, AN ITALIAN, A POLE WALK INTO A BAR . . . AND PROHIBITION BEGINS

Behr, Edward. *Prohibition: Thirteen Years That Changed America*. New York: Arcade, 2011.

Pogue, Dennis. *Founding Spirits: George Washington and the Beginnings of the American Whiskey Industry*. Buena Vista, VA: Harbour Books, 2011.

Okrent, Daniel. *Last Call: The Rise and Fall of Prohibition*. New York: Scribner, 2010.

Pacult, Paul. *American Still Life: The Jim Beam Story and the Making of the World's #1 Bourbon*. Hoboken, NJ: John Wiley & Sons, 2003.

Percy, Walker. *Signposts in a Strange Land: Essays*. New York: Picador USA, 1991.

Ellington, Duke. *Music Is My Mistress*. New York: Da Capo Press, 1973.

Hemingway, Ernest. *A Moveable Feast*. New York: Scribner, 2003.

Fitzgerald, F. Scott. "A Short Autobiography." *New Yorker*, May 25, 1929.

Carr, Virginia Spencer. *Dos Passos: A Life*. Evanston, IL: Northwestern University Press, 2004.

Blotner, Joseph. *Faulkner: A Biography*. New York: Random House, 1974.

Latham, Earl. *John D. Rockefeller: Robber Baron or Industrial Statesman*. Whitefish, MT: Kessinger Publishing, 2010.

Knoop, Todd A. *Recessions and Depressions: Understanding Business Cycles*. Santa Barbara, CA: Praeger Publishing, 2010.

CHAPTER 8: G.I. JOE GETS HIS FIRST DUI

Thompson, Peter, and Robert Macklin. *The Battle of Brisbane: Australians and the Yanks at War*. Sydney, Australia: ABC Books, 2000.

Pacult, Paul. *American Still Life: The Jim Beam Story and the Making of the World's #1 Bourbon*. Hoboken, NJ: John Wiley & Sons, 2003.

Cowdery, Charles K. *Bourbon, Straight: The Uncut and Unfiltered Story of American Whiskey*. Chicago: Made and Bottled in Kentucky, 2004.

Life, May 10, 1943.

Ullman, Edward. "Amenities as a Factor in Regional Growth." *Geographical Review*, vol. 44, no. 1 (January 1954).

McDonald, John F. *Urban America: Growth, Crisis, and Rebirth*. Armonk, NY: M. E. Sharp, 2008.

Simon, Julian L. "The Effect of Advertising on Liquor Brand Sales." *Journal of Marketing Research*, vol. 6, no. 3 (August 1969).

Lears, T. J. Jackson. "The Rise of American Advertising." *Wilson Quarterly*, vol. 7, no. 5 (winter 1983).

Ferguson, James M. "Advertising and Liquor." *Journal of Business*, vol. 40, no. 4 (October 1967).

Safire, William. *Lend Me Your Ears: Great Speeches in History*. New York: W. W. Norton & Company, 2004.

CHAPTER 9: IT'S A SMALL (BATCH) WORLD AFTER ALL
EPILOGUE: BOURBON RENEWAL

Jeansonne, Glen, David Luhrssen, and Dan Sokolovic. *Elvis Presley, Reluctant Rebel: His Life and Our Times*. Santa Barbara, CA: Greenwood, 2011.

Otfinoski, Steven. *African Americans in the Performing Arts*. New York: Facts on File, 2010.

Coleman, Rick. *Blue Monday: Fats Domino and the Lost Dawn of Rock 'n' Roll*. Cambridge, MA: Da Capo Press, 2006.

Sixx, Nikki. *The Heroin Diaries: A Year in the Life of a Shattered Rock Star*. New York: Pocket Books, 2007.

"Timothy Leary: A Candid Interview with the Controversial Ex–Harvard Professor, Prime Partisan and Prophet of LSD." *Playboy*, September 1966.

Asimov, Eric. "Bourbon's Shot at the Big Time." *New York Times*, November 28, 2007.

Pacult, Paul. *American Still Life: The Jim Beam Story and the Making of the World's #1 Bourbon*. Hoboken, NJ: John Wiley & Sons, 2003.

Passmore, Nick. "The Kings of Bourbon." Forbes.com, copyright 2006. January 30, 2013.

Samuels, Bill, Jr. *Maker's Mark: My Autobiography*. Louisville: Saber Publishing, 2000.

Garino, David P. "Maker's Mark Goes Against the Grain to Make Its Mark." *Wall Street Journal*, August 1, 1980.

Sanneh, Kelefa. "Spirit Guide: Reinventing a Great Distillery." *New Yorker*, February 11–18, 2013.

Kosar, Kevin R. *Whiskey: A Global History*. London: Reaktion Books, 2010.

Johnson, Lyndon Baines. "An Address in the Rose Garden to a Meeting of Democratic Negro and Appointed Officials from the South." *LBJ Library Speech Collection*, April 21, 1965.

Index

About the Author

DANE HUCKELBRIDGE hails from the American Middle West. He holds a degree in history as well as a certificate in Latin American studies from Princeton University. *Bourbon* is his first book, although his fiction and essays have appeared in various magazines and journals. He is currently at work on a new book on the history of beer in America. He resides in New York City.